Essentials of
Quality Management

Bruce Brocka
M. Suzanne Brocka

Professional Publishing

Select chapters were taken from *Quality Management: Implementing the Best Ideas of the Masters*, by Bruce Brocka and M. Suzanne Brocka. © Richard D. Irwin, Inc., 1992.

This publication is designed to provide accurate and authoritative information in regard to the subject matter covered. It is sold with the understanding that neither the author nor the publisher is engaged in rendering legal, accounting, or other professional service. If legal advice or other expert assistance is required, the services of a competent professional person should be sought.

From a Declaration of Principles jointly adopted by a Committee for the American Bar Association and a Committee of Publishers.

©RICHARD D. IRWIN, INC., 1993

ISBN 0-7863-0305-0

All rights reserved. No part of this publication may be reproduced, stored in a retrieval system, or transmitted, in any form or by any means, electronic, mechanical, photocopying, recording, or otherwise, without the prior written permission of the publisher.

Printed in the United States of America.

1 2 3 4 5 6 7 8 9 0 WCB 0 9 8 7 6 5 4 3

CONTENTS

PART 1 FOUNDATIONAL ISSUES

Chapter 1	What Is Quality Managment?	3
Chapter 2	Why Quality Management?	15
Chapter 3	Primary Elements of Quality Management	22
Chapter 4	Implementation	47

PART 2 QUALITY MASTERS

Chapter 5	Philip Crosby	61
Chapter 6	W. Edwards Deming	64
Chapter 7	Armand V. Feigenbaum	72
Chapter 8	Kaoru Ishikawa	77
Chapter 9	Joseph M. Juran	80
Chapter 10	Tom Peters	85
Chapter 11	Genichi Taguchi	88
Chapter 12	Historical Masters	93

PART 1

FOUNDATIONAL ISSUES

1. WHAT IS QUALITY MANAGEMENT?
2. WHY QUALITY MANAGEMENT?
3. PRIMARY ELEMENTS OF QUALITY MANAGEMENT
4. IMPLEMENTATION

CHAPTER 1

WHAT IS QUALITY MANAGEMENT?

What You Would Get From 99.9% Suppliers:
At least 20,000 wrong prescriptions per year
Unsafe drinking water one hour per month
No electricity, water, or heat for 8.6 hours per year
No phone service for 10 minutes each week
Two short or long landings at each major airport per day
500 incorrect surgical operations per week
2,000 lost articles of mail per hour

Original source unknown

DEFINITION

Quality Management or Total Quality Management (TQM) is a way to continuously improve performance at every level of operation, in every functional area of an organization, using all available human and capital resources. Improvement is addressed toward satisfying broad goals such as cost, quality, market share, schedule, and growth. Quality Management combines fundamental management techniques, existing and innovative improvement efforts, and specialized technical skills in a structure focused on continuously improving all processes. It demands commitment and discipline, and an ongoing effort. Operating at a "high level" of quality may not be adequate, as can be observed from the quote above.

Quality Management relies on people and involves everyone. Quality Management is both a philosophy and a set of guiding principles that represent the foundation of a continuously improving organization, all the processes within the organization, and the degree to which present and future needs of the customers are met.

The U.S. Department of Defense uses the following definition of Total Quality Management:

> TQM is both a philosophy and a set of guiding principles that represent the foundation of a continuously improving organization. TQM is the application of quantitative methods and human resources to improve the material and services supplied to an organization, all the processes within the organization, and the degree which the needs of the customer are met, now and in the future. TQM integrates fundamental management techniques, existing improvement efforts, and technical tools under a disciplined approach focused on continuous improvement.

Quality Management could also be defined more simply by one of the following:

> Systematically and continuously improving quality of products, service, and life using all available human and capital resources.
>
> *or*
>
> An organizationwide problem-solving and process-improving methodology.
>
> *or*
>
> A system of means to economically produce goods or services that satisfy customer requirements.

The Quality Management process includes the integration of all employees, suppliers, and customers, within the corporate environment. It embraces two underlying tenets:

- Quality Management is a capability which is inherent in your employees.
- Quality Management is a controllable process, not an accidental one.

These two notions are revolutionary compared to the strict hierarchical, authoritarian organizations that existed in the past. While there may be room for such hierarchical organizations at certain times (e.g., a military unit during war), it is not appropriate for today's and tomorrow's employees in a highly competitive, global economy.

The idea of an integrated, human-oriented systems approach to management is nothing new. W. Edwards Deming, the leading Quality Management master today, was aiding Japanese firms in implementing Quality Management principles and tools in the 1950s. Historically, such authors as Sun-Tzu (a Chinese philosopher of the 2nd century B.C.) have advocated leadership based upon human values. However, U.S. managers are still overcoming 18th-century European and American ideas regarding management, wherein the workers were literally expendable. Figure 1–1, contrasts the old and *new* views of quality. Figure 1–2 shows another way to view the old and new ways via performance.

FIGURE 1-1
Two Views of Quality

Traditional View	New View
Productivity and quality are conflicting goals.	Productivity gains are achieved through quality improvements.
Quality defined as conformance to specifications or standards.	Quality is correctly defined requirements satisfying user needs.
Quality measured by degree of non-conformance.	Quality is measured by continuous process/product improvement and user satisfaction.
Quality is achieved through intensive product inspection.	Quality is determined by product design and is achieved by effective control techniques.
Some defects are allowed if product meets minimum quality standards.	Defects are prevented through process control techniques.
Quality is a separate function and focused on evaluating production.	Quality is a part of every function in all phases of the product life cycle.
Workers are blamed for poor quality.	Management is responsible for quality.
Supplier relations are short termed and cost oriented.	Supplier relationships are long term and quality oriented.

Source: U.S. Department of Defense

FIGURE 1-2
Two Views of Quality: Performance Levels

	Old Way	New Way
Quality	Parts per hundred If it's not broken, don't fix it Inspection = quality	Parts per million Continuous improvement TQM
Employee involvement	Passive suggestion systems	Proactive quality teams
	Win-lose strategy At most one improvement per employee per year	Win-win strategy Dozen or more improvements per employee per year
Focus	Short-term profits	Long-term survival

tion, and reflection. If we truly could pick up management skill in a matter of hours, it would not be an endeavor worth devoting a career to. Quality Management is a means of empowering employees, but it also empowers the manager. Quality Management has no room for managers who manage by directive, attendance, standard operating plan, or other means of management by power or fear.

To implement these techniques is a frightening experience. Trusting employees to be capable, intelligent, and compassionate has not been normal management practice over the past 200 years of U.S. business history. The Japanese are, perhaps, the most well-known implementers of Quality Management tools and concepts, yet ironically, much of what we consider to be Japanese management techniques were developed by Americans who were generally unheeded in their own country. Quality Management is not "Japanese Management." It does not depend on a country, language, or even on the type of human resources available, as some texts on Japanese management imply. Quality Management can be successful whenever and wherever the dedication exists to incorporate it into corporate culture.

Quality Management and its empowering of the worker would seem to be at odds with both the U.S. stereotype of the Japanese as kamikaze corporate conformists, and the similar labeling of U.S. workers as incorrigible cowboys yearning for an unexplored horizon. Closer examination reveals something quite different. The Japanese environment is chaotic, cooperative and forgiving; well suited to creativity and psychological fulfillment. Workers in the United States are often preoccupied with a "the way we do things," and "cover yourself" mentality. Creativity and exploration are relegated to mysterious R&D departments. Even the American press ignores or underreports major discoveries in the scientific and engineering world. Comparative studies have shown U.S. children to be the least aware (compared to other industrial nations) in understanding basic scientific facts. Talking to school-age children reveals not a slow and stuporous group, but one that is unaware, unmotivated, and more than a bit shell-shocked. What is needed is a management approach that will unleash this latent, possibly atrophied talent, providing benefit to both the worker and the firm. The goal of Quality Management is continuous improvement, but the threshold of employee motivation and empowerment must be passed through first.

PRINCIPLES AND CONCEPTS

A Quality Management program must:

- Require dedication, commitment, and participation from top leadership.
- Build and sustain a culture committed to continuous improvement.

- Focus on satisfying customer needs and expectations.
- Involve every individual in improving his/her own work processes.
- Create teamwork and constructive working relationships.
- Recognize people as the most important resource.
- Employ the best available management practices, techniques, and tools.

The prism of Figure 1–4 illustrates the notion that Quality Management commences with the "white light" of a strategic vision which is then transformed by management dynamics, the prism, into component colors, the tools and methods needed to implement this vision.

1. Process orientation, rather than solely result-oriented orientation. By being process oriented, we can affect results in an early stage. Process orientation demands a reexamination of why things are done the way they are. Improving the quality of the process improves the quality of the result. Figure 1–5 illustrates this view.

2. Cascade the implementation and involve everyone. Quality Management will first be implemented by top leadership and flow through the management structure similar to a waterfall. This cascading deployment ensures that leaders understand, demonstrate, and can teach Quality Management principles and practices before expecting them from, and evaluating them in, their staff. The cascade effect flows to the suppliers as well.

FIGURE 1–4
Quality Management Prism

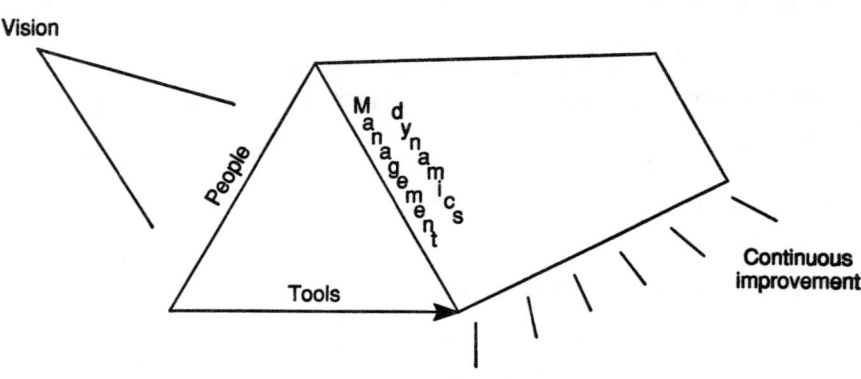

FIGURE 1-5
Process Oriented versus Results Oriented

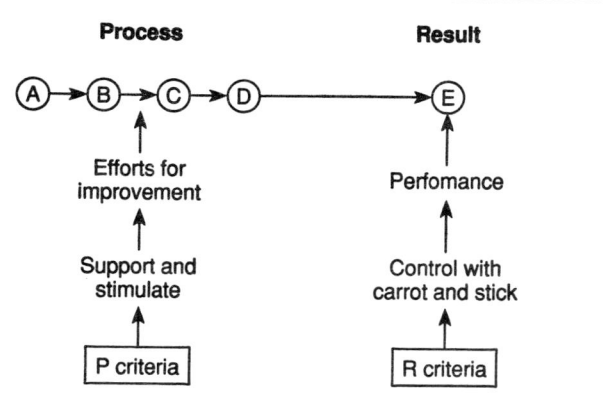

Source: Masaaki Imai, *Kaizen: The Key to Japan's Competitive Success* (New York: Random House, 1986), p. 18.

3. Commitment from top leadership. This leadership ensures strong, pervasive commitment to continuous improvement. Cost reduction, schedule compliance, customer satisfaction, and pride in workmanship all flow from an overt dedication to continuous improvement. Acting on recommendations to make positive changes demonstrates this commitment.

4. Effective, unfettered vertical and horizontal communication. Using this type of communication is essential to continuous improvement efforts. Quality Management practices aim at removing communication blocks, facilitating bidirectional communication between leaders and subordinates, and ensuring that the firm's goals and objectives are clearly delineated and disseminated throughout. A broad array of tools and techniques are available for enhancing vertical and horizontal communication. Virtually every technique in Part 3, "Management Dynamics" and Part 4, "Tools and Techniques" is communication oriented or enhancing.

5. Continuous improvement of all processes and products, internal and external. The primary Quality Management objective is an unending improvement of every aspect of one's work. That objective is implemented through a structured, disciplined approach that improves each process. With Quality Management, emphasis is placed on preventing defects through problem identification and problem-solving tools.

6. *Constancy of purpose and a shared vision.* A common purpose or set of principles must guide the organization. This can be as simple as making leakproof buckets, or as complex as the principles pervading a monastery. Whatever this purpose is, all personnel must know it and work to fulfill it. Consistency is vital; dissonant goals will result in frustration. To be courteous and informative to all callers and to process 45 calls per employee hour are goals completely at odds. When conflicting goals arise, select the higher quality alternative. In this case, eliminate the 45 calls per hour requirement, or hire the additional staff necessary to disseminate the work load reasonably.

7. *The customer is king.* The customer must rule, whether this is an internal customer (a customer is the next person in the process—internal customers are peers and supervisors) or external customer (the traditional customer). Every worker has a customer of some sort. Customers or users must be identified, and their needs, wants, expectations, and desires clearly delineated and served. Customers and their needs are the only reason a business exists.

8. *Investment in people.* Any firm's largest and most valuable investment is in its people. They are the most essential component in continuous process improvement. Training, team building, and work life enhancements are important elements in creating an environment in which employees can grow, gain experience and capability, and contribute to the firm on an ever-increasing scale. Rewards may be established, but only if it is clear to the employee what performance is expected to attain the reward, and if they are given the tools necessary to achieve this goal.

9. *Quality management begins and ends with training.* Training is constantly required for all staff. It may be to increase affective domain skills such as writing, team building concepts, or verbal skills; or it may be cognitively oriented such as statistical quality control. Training *given* today must be *used* today. Internal trainers can be invaluable, bringing a camaraderie and unique slant to the information. Unlike education, training should have an observable outcome. However, education is valuable in providing a background necessary for divergent and innovative thinking.

10. *Celebrate success and accentuate the positive.* Negative reinforcements have been found to be ineffective motivators. Establish a system of fair rewards that everyone can achieve, and everyone knows what is required to achieve the reward.

11. Two heads Are better than one. Without teamwork, Quality Management is finished before it can start. The modern team works together as a single entity, and not as a "committee" where one or a few members do or direct the work. This may require dramatic rethinking by management and employees as well. Teamwork is essential for continuous improvement. Team activities build communication and cooperation, stimulate creative thought, and provide an infrastructure supporting Quality Management practices.

12. Goal setting is communicated and determined by everyone. Employees must participate in establishing their goals. Others must be aware of goals that may impact them.

Figure 1-6 categorizes and summarizes the primary Quality Management principles. This list is not all-inclusive, but represents a distillation of many authors. These principles should be redefined and made specific for each company as it develops its own Quality Management philosophy.

The idea behind continuous improvement, or *kaizen* as the Japanese call it, is that small improvements, done continuously, will amount to major changes in an over time, and not necessarily a long period of time. Japanese manufacturing firms employing this technique during the late 1970s and early 1980s *leapfrogged* U.S. manufacturers into a position of worldwide technological dominance. Management techniques can evolve too, and Figure 1-7, from Rossier and Sink provides an evolutionary view of Quality Management. Understanding where your organization is in the evolutionary avenue will lead to an understanding of the Promethean in undertaking Quality Management.

BIBLIOGRAPHY

Ackoff, R., and F. Emery. *On Purposeful Systems*. Chicago: Aldine/Atherton, 1972.

Badiru, Adedeji B. "A Systems Approach to Total Quality Management." *Industrial Engineering* 22, no. 3 (March 1990), pp. 33-36.

Deming, W. Edwards. *Out of the Crisis*. Cambridge, Mass.: MIT Press, 1986.

Ernst & Young Quality Improvement Consulting Group. *Total Quality: An Executive's Guide for the 1990s*. Homewood, Ill.: Richard D. Irwin, 1990.

Feigenbaum, Armand V. *Total Quality Control*. New York: McGraw-Hill, 1983.

Nemoto, Masao, and David Lu, trans. and ed. *Total Quality Control for Management: Strategies and Techniques from Toyota and Toyoda Gosei*. Englewood Cliffs, N.J.: Prentice Hall, 1987.

Rossier, Paul E., and D. Scott Sink. "What's Ahead for Productivity and Quality Improvement." *Industrial Engineering* 22, no. 3 (March 1990), pp. 25-31.

FIGURE 1-6
Quality Management Principles Summary

Management Vision and Commitment

Process must begin with topmost management.
Problems often must be solved by changing or renewing the process or system.
Quality is a way of life.

Barrier Elimination

Rampant involvement, including suppliers and customers, is essential.
Yield authority to the lowest possible level to resolve problems.
Change must be the norm, not the exception.

Communication

Communication and information dissemination are vital.
Inform the end user of the information as quickly as possible.
It is more important to be clear than correct.

Continuous Evaluation and Measurement

Identify customer requirements.
Constantly use feedback.
Self-assess and reflect continuously.

Continuous Improvement

Quantify and measure.
Measure the cost of quality.
Continuously monitor vital measurements of a product.
Reduce variation.

Customer/Vendor Involvement

Customer must be king.
Vendors are part of the solution, not the problem.
Customer requirements, desires, hopes, and fears must be continuously monitored.
Customers may be internal.

Empowerment

Management style must be actively participative.
Employees must be actively involved.
Authority and autonomy must be commensurate with duties.

Training

Emphasize that long-term success is survival.
Quality is conformance to customer requirements.
Enhance skills to measure quality and identify problems.
Training must be at all levels.

FIGURE 1-7
Major Present, Emerging, and Future Improvement Strategies and Techniques

Planning	Measurement	Total Quality Management	Management of Participation	Reward System
Present: Business Facilities Capital Product	Statistical quality control. Financial ratios. Management by objectives. Performance by appraisal. Discounted cash flow. Project management. Cost accounting. Individual oriented. Tool driven. Analyst developed and maintained.	Quality assurance. Inspection. Quality circles. Statistical quality control. Streamlining. Value engineering. Buzzwords, no operational definitions. Could cost.	Quality circles. Individual suggestion systems. Education, training, and development as expense. Brainstorming. "Participative management." Task forces. Committees. Employee = workers only as used in employee involvement. Education, training, development is up front, rigid not flexible.	Incentive systems. Piece rate. Merit pay. Across-the-board-pay raises. Rigid benefits. Rewards not linked to performance. Individual focus. Profit sharing. Labor focus.
Emerging: Human resource Performance improvement Quality	Input output analysis. Statistical process control. Total factor productivity measurement model. Objectives matrix. Cost driver analysis (i.e., IBM common staffing study). Cost schedule control system. Competitive benchmarking. Management systems analysis. Decision support system.	Quality management. Assurance. Less reliance on inspection. Statistical process control. Design to production transition. Customer focus. Subcontractor/vendor control. Operational definitions TQM as buzzword.	Performance action teams. Group suggestion systems. Small-group activities. Education, training, and development as investment. Nominal group technique. "Management of participation." Employee = everyone including top management. Education, training, development is on as-needed basis, and flexible.	Gainsharing systems. Award fees. Industrial modernization incentives program. Performance based. Flexible benefits. Rewards linked to performance. Group focus. Performance improvement sharing. All factor (i.e., labor, capital, material, energy) focus
Future: Total integrated and highly participative	Total integrated measurement system. Management support systems. Improvement-oriented measurement. Statistical performance control. Total system oriented (individual, group, organization) and integrated. Management team/user driven. User developed and maintained.	Design of experiments. Quality function deployment. Real TQM = total life-cycle quality management. Total performance management.	Semiautonomous work groups, autonomous work groups. Self-managed work groups. Top-down and bottom-up strategic performance improvement planning.	Employee stock ownership. Integrated individual group and organization performance appraisal and reward systems. Total compensation system management.

Source: Paul E. and D. Scott Sink, "What's Ahead for Productivity and Quality Improvement," *Industrial Engineering* 22, no. 3 (March 1990), pp. 25–31.

Schultz, Louis E. *The Role of Top Management in Effecting Change to Improve Quality and Productivity.* Minneapolis, Minn.: Process Management Institute, 1985, pp. 1–8.

Schultz, Louis E. *Overview of Quality Management Philosophies.* Minneapolis, Minn.: Process Management Institute, 1986.

Shores, Dick. "TQC: Science, Not Witchcraft." *Quality Progress* 22, no. 4 (April 1989), pp. 42–45.

Strickland, Jack, and Peter Angiola. *Total Quality Management in the Department of Defense.* Washington, D.C.: U.S. Government Printing Office, 1989.

Strickland, Jack. "Key Ingredients to Total Quality Management." *Defense*, March/April 1989, pp. 17–21.

Sullivan, Edward, and Douglas D. Danforth. "A Common Commitment to Total Quality." *Quality Progress*, April 1986.

Tribus, M. *Deming's Redefinition of Management.* Cambridge, Mass.: MIT Press, 1985.

Tribus, M. *Reducing Deming's 14 Points to Practice.* Cambridge, Mass.: MIT Press, 1984.

Vansina, Leopold S. "Total Quality Control: An Overall Organizational Improvement Strategy." *National Productivity Review* 9, no. 1 (Winter 1989/90), pp. 59–73.

Walsh, Loren M.; Ralph Wurster; and Raymond J. Kimber, eds. *Quality Management Handbook.* New York: Marcel Dekker, 1986.

Willoughby, W. J. *Best Practices: How to Avoid Surprises in the World's Most Complicated Technical Environment.* Department of the Navy, Washington, D.C.: U.S. Government Printing Office, March 1986.

CHAPTER 2

WHY QUALITY MANAGEMENT?

For every complex question there is a simple answer, and it is wrong.

H. L. Mencken

INTRODUCTION

"My business is doing fine—Why bother with Quality Management if it's so much work?" A reasonable question, but it ignores the following:
Your product could be wiped out overnight by:

- Technology: There are no Fortune 500 candlestick makers—but everybody needed this product at one time.
- A new law: Environmental laws are squeezing more and more chemicals off the shelf, and changing the way business conducts day-to-day operations.
- A competitor's newfound superiority: The word processor WordStar® was once dominant; its market share eroded quickly when WordPerfect came on the scene and WordStar® was slow to respond.
- A change in lifestyle: Better find a way to microwave your food product, remove most of its fat, salt, cholesterol, and calories, *and* have it be as tasty as if it were prepared conventionally.

Even if your product is not threatened with extinction wouldn't you like to:

- Go from 92 percent (about one out of a dozen) defect free to 99.97 percent (one out of 3,333) defect free? Xerox did—in just six years. Their goal is no defects per million. It may be that you would have better odds in a lottery than finding a defective Xerox part.

- Cut order processing times from 55 days to 15? Motorola did.
- Reduce setup times from hours to one minute? Toyota did.
- Create, define, and dominate a market as did Fred Smith of Federal Express?
- Materialize from Bentonville, Arkansas, to challenge and eventually overtake all discount retail stores (including 100-year-old giant Sears)? Sam Walton locates most of his company's Wal-Mart stores in the sparsely populated areas of the "fly over land" of the Midwest and South.

Or do you already match the firm of the 90s that the chronicler of excellence Tom Peters describes in *Thriving on Chaos:*

> Flatter, populated by autonomous units, oriented towards product differentiation. Quality conscious, service conscious, more responsive, much faster at innovation, and a user of highly flexible people.

A number of works explore at great length the perils facing business. *Fortune, Forbes, BusinessWeek,* and *The Wall Street Journal* do so on a regular basis. A condensation of the major issues is presented in this chapter. Readers interested in either depressing or inflaming (or both) themselves should read any or all of the works referenced at the end of this chapter, or in viewing the PBS television documentary, "Quality or Else," aired in October 1991.

LESSONS FROM HISTORY

In their mesmerizing work, *American Business: A Two-Minute Warning,* Grayson and O'Dell offer 10 lessons from the history of leading economic nations (leader) and newly industrialized nations (challengers) that can guide our motivation in adopting Quality Management:

1. Complacency is the cancer of leadership.
2. Leaders overlook growth rates of challengers.
3. The growth rates are small and incremental, and not realized until too late.
4. Size is a poor estimator of success.
5. Challengers have the "eye of the tiger" (desire), the leaders have lost it.
6. Challengers stress education and improvement; leaders chop training when the budget gets tight.

7. Challengers copy strategies; leaders find it beneath them.
8. Challengers are customer oriented, leaders become producer oriented.
9. Protectionism hurts leaders and helps challengers.
10. The leader's ability to change and respond wanes with time.

LESSONS FROM TODAY

A survey of 700 British CEOs by Lascelles and Barrie found the following motivators for quality improvement programs:

- Demanding customers—73 percent
- Need to reduce costs—63 percent
- CEO initiative—59 percent
- Competitors—34 percent

They also discovered the disconcerting fact that personnel in fewer than half of what the companies surveyed had received training in Quality Management techniques. Not surprisingly, it would seem that customers are driving the need for continuous improvement. There are also societal factors that motivate us to find new ways to conduct work as the needs and expectations of new generations emerge.

The U.S. Government Accounting Office (GAO), the investigative service of Congress, analyzed 20 of the highest scoring companies applying for the Malcolm Baldrige National Quality Award (Chapter 18, section "Benchmarking") and found the following benefits from instituting quality management:

- Quality improved and costs decreased. Reliability and on-time delivery increased; errors, lead time, and complaints were reduced.
- Customer satisfaction increased, and the overall perception of quality increased.
- Profitability and market share increased. Quality Management practices lead to improved profitability.
- Employee relations improved somewhat. Absenteeism and turnover was reduced, and employees experienced increased job satisfaction.

The GAO found the following distinctive features of the Quality Management efforts:

- Attention focused on meeting customer requirements.
- Senior management demonstrates quality values by incorporating them into daily operations.
- Systematic processes promoting continuous improvement were woven through the organization.
- Training and empowering processes were instrumental in quality improvement efforts.

The GAO also found that the performance improvement efforts required about 2.5 years.

MODERN FORCES

Just as classrooms have changed from places where reading, writing, and arithmetic were taught to school systems that provide for the health, education, welfare, and well-being of their charges, so has the work force needed to evolve from a place to earn a wage for food and shelter into a complex socioeconomic system. Workers now seek fulfillment from their work, not just a paycheck. The transformation of the work force is made even more difficult by the forces of global competition, technological change, environmental change, social forces, and changing work ethics. These external forces are changing forever the way in which we conduct business.

The effect of these forces is not magically cured by Quality Management, but Quality Management will allow all available company resources to develop alternatives to mitigate the impacts. Some of these forces may demand Quality Management as part of their resolution.

Global Competition

In the past, lack of communication and education often made possible a company's success. Markets of broad scope could be targeted with little thought to unknown or small competitors. Today, competition is truly global. One never knows who or where the next competitor will be. Quality Management aids in anticipating competition by continuously striving for quality improvements; there is no room for complacent leadership. For example, in the same quarter, three major computer manufacturers (IBM, Apple, and Compaq) announced difficulties in coping with what they saw as a flat marketplace, while at least three upstart companies (Dell, Zeos, and Gateway) announced another recordbreaking quarter of sales.

Technological Change

The very foundations of how and why we do what we do will change in ways unknown to us now. Yet these forces can wipe out an entire mature industry in a few years (e.g., compact discs versus vinyl record albums). The older adult generation of today may in fact have more in common with the writers of ancient papyri than with the nearly illiterate future world of audiovisual images. If this seems unlikely to you, consider the following:

- Videotaped courtroom proceedings as legal record.
- Fast-food cash registers with keys representing the food (no numbers).
- Videotaped high school yearbooks.
- Universal traffic symbols.
- Videos outsell books four to one.

There does not seem to be a technology plateau in sight; new generations of computer hardware that used to appear every three to five years, to every two years, are now appearing about every 10 to 12 months.

Quality Management reduces turbulence caused by new technology by embracing it, rather than ignoring it. New technology can be stimulating and is constantly opening new business opportunities. What would the state of American business be today if it were not for its seminal and dominant (or codominant) role in computer hardware and software technology?

Social Forces

We spend many of our waking hours at our workplace, and several more hours preparing, commuting, and thinking about our work. For most adults between the ages of 21 and 65, work is the primary feature of their life. We may get married, divorced, have custody of children for shorter or longer times, but during that span, we are almost always employed. With such a focus, it is not surprising that people look to work for fulfillment and enrichment; some may even find a calling in their work. Quality Management can provide the galvanizing impulse that an organization needs to provide management that dissipates frustrations, and capitalizes upon the pent-up energy of its work force.

The social fabric has been torn—the evidence assails us in the daily newspapers:

- Children without fathers are rapidly becoming a social norm, even a majority. Women who head single parent households are generally living in poverty as are their children.

- Twenty-three percent of the children in the United States under the age of six live in poverty.
- The United States spends more on social security for elderly who have incomes of over $50,000 per year than we do for the entire food stamp program.
- Manipulative "information" from broadcast and print media cheats viewers and readers of realistic views of how life should be lived.

Thus it is little wonder, then, that the typical worker trudges into work embittered, his mind wandering to anything except the tasks before him. Quality Management cannot fix any of these problems, but it can help to provide a workplace where humane and honest treatment can be found, and perhaps provide a measure of fulfillment.

Work Ethic

The value of work is praised in countries that are economically successful regardless of the era. Germans pride themselves on their discipline. So do the Japanese. Work ethic used to be equated with loyalty to a company in the United States. This has changed. The new breed of professional feels loyal to their discipline (mechanical engineering, accounting, writing, and so on), not to any company. It may be easy to misinterpret this new work ethic. It manifests itself in workers seeking new projects and opportunities, and having authority over these projects. The old conformance work ethic operated under a code of unquestioning obeisance, stifling creativity and optimum performance.

Work value cannot be directed from the CEO or a minister. It stems from the powerful force of peer values. Peer values are not limited to human-to-human interaction. Television, for example, can exert a considerable influence, since we average some 20 to 40 hours per week watching it. Quality Management can provide a work atmosphere that nurtures a work ethic and allows workers to achieve their potential as workers as well as humans. The president of Johnsonville Sausage, Ralph Stayer, says that it is immoral (a rare word these days) not to allow workers to reach their full potential, at least while on the job. Rigid hierarchies that allow no questioning and teamwork are demeaning, and criminally waste the human resources of society. However, the message is often the opposite of this ideal: CEO compensation ratios to that of a laborer can be as high as 9,000:1.[1] When a society values individuals solely on income, it is easy to see that the breakdown of societal values has either happened or is looming.

---

[1] Steven Ross, CEO of Time Warner, received $78 million in total compensation in 1990. "Corporate America's Most Powerful People," *Forbes*, May 27, 1991.

The work ethic prescribes perseverance. In an era of 44-minute life-and-death decisions (the actual length of most hour-long television shows), apparently instant riches with no evident physical or mental effort, it is understandable why perseverance is an anachronism.

The work ethic problem affords Quality Management a great challenge, as it cannot be controlled outside of the workplace, where many attitudes are formed. A company can, nevertheless, provide examples and reward individuals who display such a work ethic. A corporate culture cannot entirely supplant an external culture, however, it can reshape attitudes and reinforce positive traits from the external culture.

If the above forces have not been sufficient to stimulate a desire to engage in a Quality Management program, then consider that your competitor is probably instituting just such an approach, viewing it as a necessary means for survival. Quality Management is not the simple answer to the problems facing management, but it can be the right one.

BIBLIOGRAPHY

Bennis, Warren. "The Coming Death of Bureaucracy." *Think* 32 (November/December 1966), pp. 30–35.

Bhote, Keri. "America's Quality Health Diagnosis: Strong Heart, Weak Head." *Management Review,* May 1989.

Brown, J. H. U., and J. Comola. *Educating for Excellence: Improving Quality and Productivity in the 90's.* New York: Auburn House, 1991.

Dobyns, Lloyd, and Clare Crawford-Mason. *Quality or Else.* Boston: Houghton Mifflin, 1991.

Drucker, Peter F. "The Coming of the New Organization." *Harvard Business Review,* January/February 1988, pp. 45–53.

Drucker, Peter F. *The New Realities.* New York: Harper & Row, 1989.

Grayson, C. J., and C. O'Dell. *American Business—A Two-Minute Warning: Ten Tough Issues Managers Must Face.* New York: Free Press, 1988.

Harrington, H. James. *Excellence—The IBM Way.* Milwaukee, Wis.: ASQC Quality Press, 1988.

Lascelles, David, and Barrie Dale. "Quality Management: The Chief Executive's Perception and Role." *Journal of European Management* 8, no. 1 (March 1990), pp. 67–75.

Townsend, Patrick L., and Joan A. Gebhardt. *Commit to Quality.* New York: John Wiley & Sons, 1990.

U.S. Government Accounting Office. NSIAD 91-190, as reported in *On Q,* September 1991.

CHAPTER 3

PRIMARY ELEMENTS OF QUALITY MANAGEMENT

My mistake was buying stock in the company.
Now I worry about the lousy work I'm turning out.

Marvin Townsend

The "Pillars of TQM" or the primary elements of Quality Management philosophy vary from author to author, and their number may vary, but their marrow is the following:

1. Organizational vision.
2. Barrier removal.
3. Communication.
4. Continuous evaluation.
5. Continuous improvement.
6. Customer/vendor relationships.
7. Empowering the worker.
8. Training.

This set was selected because it applies to organizations initially making the move to a Quality Management program. As organizations advance, training, barrier removal, and communication can be subsumed into empowering the worker. Continuous evaluation and continuous improvement could perhaps be combined into continuous analysis.

Thus distilled, this leaves us with four essential ingredients from which the other concepts flow. These concepts are presented in Figure 3–1. These components make up the strategic portion of the quality pyramid developed by Ronald Snee in Figure 3–2. The managerial aspects are detailed in Part 3, and the operational aspects may be found in Part 4. Chapter 4, "Implementation,"

FIGURE 3-1
Four Key Components

Top-down strategic vision demonstrated daily via leadership
Continuous analysis and product/service improvement
Empower and liberate employees
Listen and react to customers and vendors

FIGURE 3-2
Quality Management Pyramid

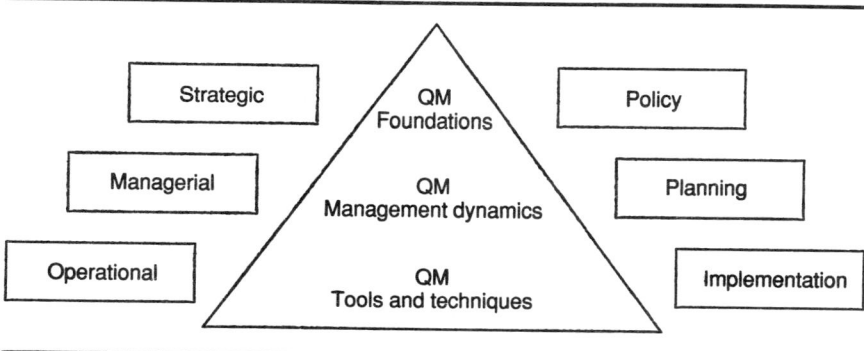

relates to the strategic, managerial, and operational elements. Each of the eight foundational elements is discussed below.

1. ORGANIZATIONAL VISION

Organizational vision provides the framework that guides a firm's beliefs and values. This can be as simple as "making the best widgets at the lowest cost to the consumer," or as structured as the organizational culture of IBM. The gist of the corporate vision should be a simple, one sentence guide or motto that every employee knows, and more important, believes. If well crafted, the vision statement (which is typically one paragraph to no more than two pages) can serve through a torrent of change in product and service technology. For example, if you were a coach builder in the year 1910, and decided that you made the finest horse coaches available, the subsequent decade or two would have bankrupted you. If you had decided that you provided fine coach work, irrespective of the driving engine, you may have adapted quickly to the new challenges. Technology is rapidly making many things obsolete. Broad vision state-

FIGURE 3-3
The General Motors Quality Network Process Model

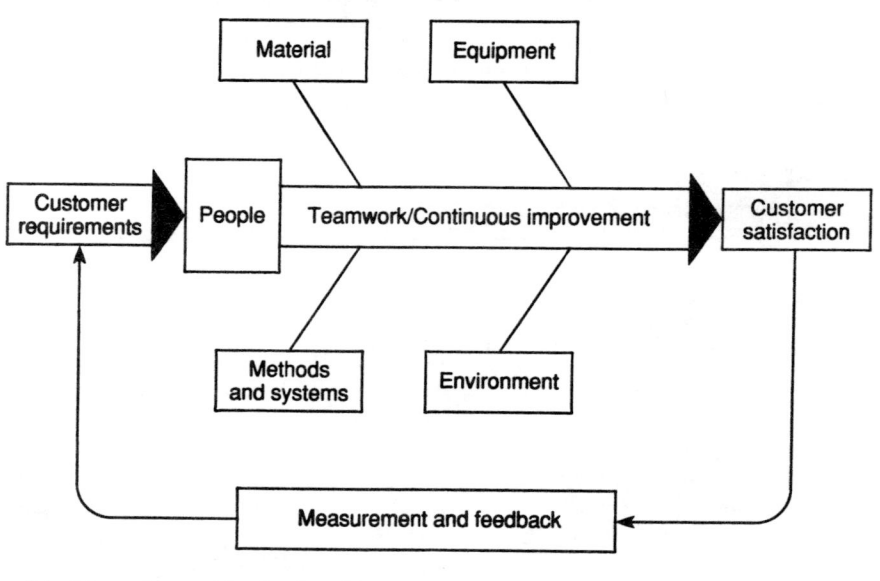

A tool to analyze, understand, and improve any process.

ments are now the norm, although this sometimes leads to such stilted phrases as "music delivery system" for audiotapes, CDs, and videos of musicians.

General Motors provides all employees a card with its strategic vision, including a cause-effect diagram indicating the teamwork necessary. This card is reproduced in Figure 3-3. John Hartley, CEO of Harris Corporation, formulated this statement:

> Harris must be perceived as a company of the highest quality in every aspect of its business activity.
> This would seem rather broad, although Harris makes an incredibly diverse array of products.

This strategic vision needs to consider both the external customer and the internal customer, or the employees, but lacks a defining or differentiating phrase. We all like to be the best but this needs to be combined with a goal such as "fastest to market" or "lowest cost," or some other distinguishing phrase. As younger, more consumer-oriented workers gain dominance in the work force, a firm's identity, ethics, and beliefs will become increasingly important to the work force and shareholders alike. A sense of purpose must guide our actions if our lives are to have any sense of meaning and fulfillment. In the past, the utility of the work we did was subsumed by an external goal. We did the work to bring ourselves or our children out of poverty. The work could be degrading because our survival was at risk. This is no longer the case in most businesses, as in many areas of the world. We are ascending Maslow's hierarchy of needs[1] from the survival stage and are nearer the actualization stage. As work occupies most people's waking hours, it is only logical for them to seek fulfillment while on the job. This does not (necessarily) translate to the need to implement all manner of costly *wellness* programs, but presents a need to let the work force know that what they do is important and vital to the community in some way.

Simply stating a vision is not enough. It needs to be demonstrated by the actions of the executives, managers, supervisors, foremen, and individuals. It is done continuously in all of their actions and initiatives. Employees know the difference between an "open-door" policy and a "slightly ajar" actuality.

Deliberation must be exercised in developing these goals and strategies. They must reflect the values and culture of the work force. While top-management commitment is essential, it is also essential to know when to lead and when to get out of the way (the old saw, "If they throw you out of town, make it look like a parade," has relevancy here). In a sense, Quality Management is management from the bottom up, as latent talents are coaxed out. Quality must be infused into all processes the organization engages in, whether it is managerial, administrative, functional, or some other process. An atmosphere must be created in which each individual feels responsible to the customer for whatever product is produced or service rendered, and a responsibility exists to the customer, whether that customer is internal or external to the organization. This may well require a gut-wrenching change in the way day-to-day business is conducted.

Inspiring an Organizational Vision

While a vision or mission statement is a product of the strategic vision process, unless it is transformed into action, the statement is useless. There are four keys to successful vision implementation:

1. Total involvement. Every level of the organization, including senior management, must be involved in quality improvement activities.

2. Communication. It is essential that everyone in the organization understand the specifications of his or her customers, and be conscious of how well he or she is meeting the customers' needs.

---

[1] Maslow developed a hierarchy of needs ranging from food and shelter to family needs to "self-actualization" or spiritual enlightenment. This hierarchy is illustrated in Figure 3–10.

FIGURE 3-4
Strategies in Successful Vision Implementation

Demonstrate commitment.	Inform suppliers.
Maintain a constancy of purpose.	Take a long-term view.
Create more leaders.	Establish meaningful goals.
Examine your mission.	Discuss TQM with peers.
Behavior and actions must be consistent with goals.	Build awareness.

3. Barrier removal. Structures, policies, and procedures must be implemented to encourage quality. All those that restrict progress toward Quality Management must be removed. Quality Management must be part of the strategic plan, the budget process, and the employee reward system. Barrier removal is the first step in empowering employees. Constantly ask why it should be done this way, and constantly ask why am I deciding this, versus the people directly involved.

4. Continuously improve and evaluate. Keep looking for a better way, even if your customers are satisfied with the current product or service. Quality improvement can be the ultimate integrator of the organization, helping to achieve critical Quality Management objectives: improved product quality, lower costs, stronger customer loyalty, increased employee morale and lower unwanted turnover.

2. BARRIER REMOVAL

It is inevitable that change will be resisted. In fact, a great deal of effort in Quality Management is expended in overcoming such resistance, usually by allowing change to come from individuals directly involved, rather than as a directive from management. The whole idea of continuous improvement leads to continuous change. Ideas for adapting to this change are discussed in Chapter 13, section on Change Management. This section will focus on overcoming barriers associated with the implementation of the continuous improvement process.

The following strategies are recommended throughout the barrier removal process:

- Drive out fear.
- Encourage and reward creative thinking—even if the ideas are not implemented.
- Share the credit for success.
- Revise and renew performance measurement systems.

FIGURE 3-5
Some Common Barriers

We know what they really want (without asking them).
Quality is not a major factor in decisions—low initial cost mentality prevails.
Creative accounting can increase corporate performance.
Can't manufacture competitively at the low end.
The job of senior management is strategy, not operations.
Success is good, failure is bad.
If it ain't broke, don't fix it.
The key disciplines from which to draw senior management are finance and marketing.
Increase in quality means increase in cost.
Thinking that time, quality, cost are at worst mutually exclusive, at best we can only choose two out of three.

- Justify cost over the life cycle, not just initial cost.
- Establish ownership of tasks and projects.

The following are the steps to barrier removal:

1. Identify barriers. Anything that stands in the way of implementing and realizing continuous improvement should be considered a barrier. This means examining internal procedures, customer relations and concerns, and personnel issues. Anything that is perceived to be a barrier deserves further consideration. At this initial stage, no judgment as to priority or validity should be made. Generation of the list can be accomplished by several of the techniques described in Part 4 "Tools and Techniques." Perhaps brainstorming (Chapter 19) would be the most effective at this stage. David A. Nadler of Delta Consulting group provided the examples of corporate culture barriers listed in Figure 3-5 during a Xerox Quality Education Seminar.

2. Place into categories. Related barriers and their systemic causes may now be analyzed. Validity judgment should still be held in abeyance at this stage. Categorization may be facilitated by using cause-effect diagrams or other organizing tools (Chapter 16). Be alert for barriers that mask or cause one another. It is not unusual for a myriad of problems to be caused by a few difficulties. Quality function deployment is another useful technique that may be used in conjunction with, or instead of cause-effect diagrams.

3. Establish priority. This should be done by using a tool such as Pareto analysis (Chapter 20), cause-effect diagrams, or by the Delphi technique (Chapter 19). Care must be taken to establish an objective process, whatever that process might be. It should not be influenced by management, or by a hidden agenda. At this stage barriers are judged on their validity in accordance with the severity of the problem. It can be difficult to compare relative barriers at this stage, if a common denominator, such as dollars or number of defective units is not used. In companywide searches for barriers, it may be necessary to find more than one denominator and deal with the problem accordingly.

4. Problem solve. This means more than symptom removal! In medicine, symptom alleviation allows the patient to think that he is cured, even though the patient, if untreated, will recover in the same amount of time, or may not recover at all. Sick organizations do not recover for the long term if symptoms are masked. At best, symptom masking makes one quarter's report better. Akio Morita, chairman of Sony corporation, has chastised American managers for planning ahead for only 10 minutes rather than 10 years.

It is vital to address the root cause of the problem. By using cause-effect diagrams and quality function deployment it may become apparent that the elimination of one barrier may solve many problems. Do not be surprised if this "master cause" looks intractable, such as "poor communication among management and workers." These "soft" problems are the ones that plague us for years, and may take years to solve. While this sounds expensive to cure, be assured that the competition will ultimately solve any such long-term illnesses for you. Analysis of the problem should include estimates of resources required for its resolution. A cause-effect diagram or force field analysis will be useful in identifying the nature of the solutions, and potential hindrances in successful problem resolution.

5. Goals and strategies for resolution. Resolution of problems may entail goals over a period of months or years. Goals should be realistic and attainable with the given resources. Strategies ensure that goals can be accomplished. Bear in mind that numerical goals as such may not be what is required. A 15 percent improvement with no strategy is meaningless, if not insulting. Numerical goals may also limit the amount of growth, particularly in organizations used to working up to an "average," as occurs in many piecework situations. Allowing people to work to their optimum, without harming other workers, will provide measurable improvements without numerical quotas. Attaining a short-term goal may be possible by altering the natural rhythm of a process, but may not be workable over an extended period of time.

Who Should Do This?

The general supposition is that volunteers in a cross-functional team should identify proposed solutions for barrier removal. No one should be tasked to do it. However, in the early stages of Quality Management implementation, a valuable individual may ignore such a call for volunteers, having been beaten down by the existing system. This person may need to be asked. If he refuses, he should not be co-opted. As Quality Management is implemented properly, this type of volunteer problem goes away. People see that they can indeed make a difference. A balance should be achieved among departments, that is, shop floor versus nonshop floor workers, and so on. Do not consider an area where representation is not present. Do not suppose that union workers necessarily have a built-in adversarial role, or that less-educated workers will be unable to articulate their concerns and analyze problems. After all, a union electrical worker has led Poland into a new era of social democracy that embraces capitalism.

3. COMMUNICATION

Communication is the glue that binds all of the techniques, practices, philosophies, and tools. Ineffective communication will doom the most clever of Quality Management initiatives. Communication may be: written, verbal, or nonverbal. Understanding and refining skills for each of the main types of communication is an ongoing process for everyone. Recurring training in each of the areas is a must to develop and retain communication skills.

All forms of communication involve four elements: the sender, the receiver, the message, and the medium. The medium is the method of delivery, and can influence the message. One pop media guru of the 1960s declared that "the medium was the message," referring in part to the hypnotic entrancement of television. Because of the filtering effects that can happen to a message (Figure 3–6), it is important to understand how communication works, and how personality factors influence our understanding. An excellent method on understanding cross-generational differences is Massey's idea of *what you are now is what you were when*. His thesis is that people are value programmed by 10 years of age, and that understanding the receiver's value system relative to the sender's value system is vital. For example, someone who turned 10 during the Depression would view a situation differently than someone who grew up during the more comfortable 50s. Understanding how past experiences color present situations can overcome the differences in value systems, one of the most difficult to overcome barriers listed in Figure 3–6.

Written Communication
Principally the domain of office workers, written skills take decades to hone. Office memos and reports are often the results of hundreds of hours (studies indicate anywhere from 21 percent to 70 percent of office workers' time is spent manipulating written information) of work, and their final form should be worthy of spending some time to get the words right. Shun bureaucratic

FIGURE 3-6
Barriers to Communicating Effectively

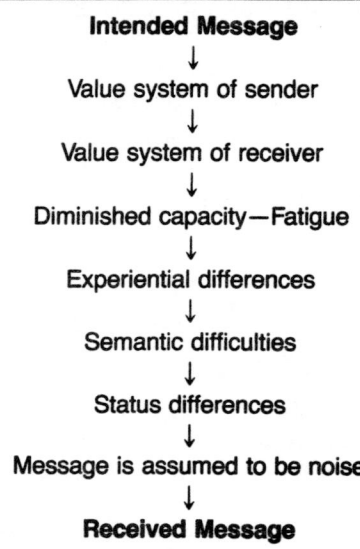

language and write in the active voice as much as possible when preparing memos and reports. The use of white space and graphical elements such as figures and charts enhances the readability of any written piece. The ability to write is directly correlated with reading. The more we read, the better our writing becomes. Given the vast amount of time spent on reading and creating memos, letters, proposals, and the like, the byword on written communication should be more is better, and the less permanent (memos sent electronically, faxes, hand notes on the bottom of letters, rather than a typed, recorded reply) the better.

Verbal
Verbal communication takes place in a variety of settings, and the form of the communication will vary. One sort of vocabulary may be used in addressing shareholders; a different idiom may be used altogether when chatting with the loading dock crew. The skills principally lacking in verbal communication are:

- Public speaking.
- Small group interaction.

Public speaking scares people more than death, if one believes the *Book of Lists*. This fear is not ameliorated by speaking to a group of known peers.

In fact, it can be worse. Three things can help overcome the fear of public speaking:

Training provides the framework for developing a public or small group speech. Organization and practice are essential ingredients in preparing a presentation.

Videotaping of presentations may be embarrassing, so allow the speech giver to review the videotape in private, with the reviewer's comments in a written form. Videotaping makes abundantly clear every "and-umm, uhhh, and y'know." Alternative means of alleviating stress may need to be developed.

Practice. Join a group such as Toastmasters that requires regular public speaking in a friendly environment. As confidence grows, so does ability.

Small group interaction is not always identified as a separate type of speech, but when implementing the myriad Quality Management tools that require teams, it is vital to understand how small groups interact. Small groups are discussed in Chapter 14, section on "Team Building" and Chapter 19, "Group Techniques."

Nonverbal
Humans infer a great deal of information from nonverbal clues. This nonverbal information includes *body language* as well as such things as *dress for success*. Anthropologists have discovered that human emotions are registered on the face in the same way, irrespective of cultural origin. Nonverbal clues lead to "gut feels" about the how to interact with another person. Despite the similarities of nonverbal communication, there are cultural differences, and is probably most important to understand these, rather than "reading" an individual's body language. It is easy to fall into the trap of overanalyzing nonverbal clues and infusing them with meaning, when, for example, someone may simply be hard of hearing or near/far-sighted rather than being inattentive (or too attentive).

Conflict Resolution
Communication can be the cause and cure of conflicts that arise. A conflict resolution process needs to identify the problem by identifying the who, what, why, when, and how, of each side, and treat both complaints as legitimate. Determine the common goal and causes. What are the underlying interests of each party? A root cause should be searched for, as there may be a systemic problem. An approach to solving the dispute must then be described, being as fair as possible to both sides. A facilitator may be required to aid in the conflict resolution. Most organizations have formal resolution mechanisms available, but have few or no informal mecha-

nisms. An ombudsman or designated facilitator may assist in resolving conflicts prior to their reaching a point where a formal process is required.

4. CONTINUOUS EVALUATION

Feedback is essential to continuous improvement. How else would we know if our goals are coming to fruition or if the variation has been reduced? How else can we implement corrective action in a timely fashion? It is too late to find after the scheduled completion date that the project has run aground. These feedback mechanisms may be simple oral or written reports, information systems, or complex automated statistical analyses integrated with expert systems. The key is to receive the information in time to allow initiating corrective action.

Not only is it important to have timely information, but to deliver that information to someone who can initiate action. In a manufacturing envi-

FIGURE 3–7
Improvement versus Innovation

	Continuous Improvement	*Innovation*
Effect	Long term and long lasting but undramatic.	Short term, but dramatic.
Pace	Small steps.	Big steps.
Time frame	Continuous and incremental.	Intermittent and nonincremental.
Change	Gradual and constant.	Abrupt and volatile.
Involvement	Everybody.	Select few "champions."
Approach	Collectivism, group efforts, systems approach.	Rugged individualism, individual ideas and efforts.
Mode	Maintenance and improvement.	Scrap and rebuild.
Spark	Conventional know-how and state of the art.	Technological breakthroughs, new inventions, new theories.
Practical requirements	Requires little investment but great effort to maintain it.	Requires large investment but little effort to maintain it.
Effort orientation	People.	Technology.
Evaluation criteria	Process and efforts for better results.	Results for profits.
Advantage	Works well in slow-growth economy.	Better suited to fast-growth economy.

Source: Masaaki Imai, *Kaizen* (New York: Random House, 1986), p. 24.

ronment, this means access to quality control information by shop floor workers, not quality inspectors. How can the inspectors correct the problem? Certainly they can assist in the design and analysis of control charts, but they have no direct responsibility for product manufacture. It is essential to supply the shop floor worker real-time information to correct or prevent defects. Summaries and trends should also be analyzed by the shop floor worker, as well as by quality control, manufacturing engineering, and management.

Be sure to understand and separate assignable causes from chance causes. Assignable causes have distinct reasons for their existence. Chance causes are those causes over which we have no control. The employee can hardly be blamed for chance causes. Be sure of what you are trying to measure. It is unrealistic to tell the clerk to service 20 employees an hour, and provide quality service to all, no matter what it takes. What if "no matter what it takes" requires more than three minutes? The worker must not be demeaned while implementing, revamping, or evaluating a performance measurement tool.

Models of feedback can be based upon the Shewhart or Deming wheel (Chapter 17).

5. CONTINUOUS IMPROVEMENT

Engineers often employ a process called *derating* to achieve superior reliability when designing electronic devices. The idea is to select a component that can more than handle the rated voltage and operating conditions, but not greatly add to the cost of manufacture. The idea is similar to one in bodybuilding: it is easier, and more effective, to lift 50 pounds 10 times, than to move 500 pounds all at once! Continuous improvement is similar; small improvements done continuously arrive at the same point as a major innovation.[2]

Unlike innovation, which can require great resources, and no small amount of serendipity, continuous improvement is easier to manage and utilizes everyone's talents. Japanese companies have used this idea for some time, and call this approach *kaizen*. This idea fits hand in hand with team building approaches such as quality circles and brainstorming, and can be inexpensively managed. *Kaizen* and innovation are compared in Figure 3-8.

---

[2]There are two types of innovation. One type fills in the missing pieces of a "knowledge matrix." The other type of innovation overturns the matrix entirely, and asks very different questions. Einstein's theory of relativity was an innovation of the second kind. Refinements to this theory are of the first kind. The sort of innovation treated here is of the first kind. Highly creative and divergent thinking is required for the second kind, which should be cultivated, but is perhaps not as important to daily business operations as the first sort of innovation.

Traditionally, in a manufacturing environment, a quality control department inspects products against a set of requirement specifications. In a service or white-collar setting this function is often performed by an audit organization. After such inspections, defective items (or reports) may then have to be either scrapped or reworked. This sequential processing leads to quality issues being addressed after the fact. The damage has already been done; a defective product or service is completed. Time to correct the problem must now be invested — time that should have been spent doing it right the first time.

In software development it has been shown that the cost to correct an error increases exponentially with the life-cycle phase. This means that to correct a requirements error after deployment costs 100 times (or more) than to correct the error when it occurred. Quality is, therefore, achieved at increased cost and decreased productivity, the antithesis of Quality Management.

To reduce cost and increase productivity, the focus must be projected on the process that produces the product. Improving the process reduces or eliminates variation and increases the uniformity of the product. This results in lower costs through the reduction of scrap, rework, and complexity. This method applies to administrative processes also — a report format may be reused, one spreadsheet may serve many different departments. Process improvement involves everyone in the organization and becomes a part of everyone's job, rather than the responsibility of just a few members of the organization. Through the inspection and analysis of the process, everyone shares a common learning experience and the accumulated knowledge and understanding of the process become the basis for improving it. Figure 3-8 contains 10 precepts of quality improvement by Motiska and Schilliff.

Strategies

Some strategies to bear in mind when implementing continuous improvement are:

Start with an example project. Small is beautiful when initiating radical new ideas into the workplace. Prove that it can work in a department of a division before exporting it companywide.

Analyze variation of all processes. This means administrative as well as on the production line. Are quarterly reports constantly being reinvented? Develop and use templates as much as possible.

Recognize the process, not just results. How can results be changed if we ignore the process? The process is the key to improving the results.

FIGURE 3-8
Ten Precepts of Quality Improvement

1. Quality leadership must begin with top management.
2. The most important aspect of the quality process is identifying the activities within the organization that affect quality.
3. Written procedures are one of the necessary communications media by which the management functions of directing and controlling are exercised.
4. One of the most critical activities in quality improvement is preparing a clear, concise description of the product or service to be acquired or produced.
5. The cost, time, and effort devoted to evaluating and selecting suppliers must be commensurate with the importance of the goods or services to be procured.
6. Quality audits must determine the adequacy of, and compliance with, established policies, procedures, instructions, specifications, codes, standards, and contractual requirements. Quality audits must also assess the effectiveness of their implementation.
7. The simple objective of most quality audits is to gather enough reliable data through inspection, observation, and inquiry to make a reasonable assessment of the quality of the activity being audited.
8. The foundation of quality control is having timely and accurate information so that systems that are not capable of producing consistent quality can be identified and improved.
9. An effective quality cost program can help the management team allocate strategic resources for improving quality and reducing costs.
10. Productivity, profit, and quality are the ultimate measures of the success of the production system. However, it is impossible to increase productivity, profit, and quality in the long run without exemplary programs for human resources.

Source: Paul J. Motiska and Karl Shilliff, "10 Precepts of Quality," *Quality Progress* 23, no. 2 (February 1990), pp. 27–28.

Simplify, simplify, simplify. Thoreau's injunction is truer today than it was in the mid-19th century. Constantly ask what is the value added for each work step, each form, and each line on the form.

Expect to constantly reinvest in new technology. Things don't stay done anymore. This may be why women managers are beginning to excel in the work force. Traditionally, "women's tasks" are never finished—laundry, cooking, child rearing are all ongoing. There is no real notion of being finished with a task. "Men's tasks" traditionally stay done and have a definite end point—fixing the car, bagging the meat, painting the house. Like traditional women's work, business today is messy—there is no end point, no time to relax.

Failures and problems are opportunities. Perfection is boring—there is no opportunity to learn new things. We learn from our mistakes as individuals, and we can learn from organizational mistakes as well. Be stubborn—make the same mistake several times before moving on. The typical entrepreneur starts and fails at two to three enterprises before finding the right match. Restaurants also fail at a given location at about the same rate before an appropriate match to the location is made.

Reorganize in order to bring about improvement. If the strategies advocated are too difficult to bring about under the current organizational structure, a change in organization may be needed. Self managing teams may need to be established, and layers of middle managers reduced.

6. CUSTOMER/VENDOR RELATIONSHIPS

The "hearing the voice of the customer" has become a key phrase in the past five years. That companies could do anything other than listen closely to customers' needs may puzzle casual observers of business. It would seem to be an obvious point. To many American companies, however, it is not. After World War II, the United States was the only major country that did not have a devastated economic infrastructure. Therefore, we could produce items of any quality and sell them. The needs of the customer seemed irrelevant, and industries were internally driven, and not customer oriented, or customer driven.

As other players have entered the field, management styles did not adapt. This reached crisis proportions in the 1970s and 1980s. Large companies take a very long time to change. Deming compares it to turning around a very large ship, and estimates it will take America about 30 years to change. Listening to the customer requires listening throughout a product life cycle, from requirements definition to maintenance after the sale. The customer also means anyone to whom you give your work, whether or not it is a "public" customer. This greatly broadens the scope of the "customer" and assessing "customer satisfaction." Listening to the customer entails surveys, research, and the implementation of tools such as quality function deployment.

Consumer research can be made very difficult by the inability of the customer or user to articulate and separate wants, needs, and desires. Even performing such research does not guarantee stellar success. Who can predict such successes in the children's toy market such as Cabbage Patch Kids dolls, Barbie dolls, and Teenage Mutant Ninja Turtles®? Yet there is always a niche to be found and money to be made even if your product does not get splashed on the front page of the newspaper's *Lifestyles* section. Little Tikes® toy company makes high-quality products that are useful although not exactly glamorous—but they are likely to stay in business for a long time, if they actively pursue their niche. Uncontrolled growth does not equate to unlimited profits.

Some strategies for improving customer and vendor relations are:

- Link organizational vision to customer satisfaction.
- Reward suppliers.
- Move to single sourcing.
- Minimize the overall number of vendors.
- Identify internal and external customers.
- Identify end users and distributors.
- Establish routine dialogue with customers.
- Involve the customer in planning and development.

Become a Customer of Your Own Product or Service

If practical, the employee who provides a service or product should also be a customer, if only for a short time. This means that administrative employees should understand how their reports are going to be used, and they should understand how the product works. A small arms unit of the Canadian Army had all of its personnel, including civilian administrative staff, take a course in firing and maintaining the weapon. This increased the ability of the staff to respond to questions and the secretaries could better proofread correspondence, since they now had an idea of the meaning of the content. All employees should be part of an enthusiastic (and un-co-opted) sales force.

Vendors Are Partners

Procurement systems spend some 60 percent of the sales dollar, and therefore is 60 percent of the quality problem or solution. By viewing purchasing as a strategic function, procurement becomes an essential link in the Quality Management chain. Most Quality Management coaches advise reducing the number of suppliers, and establishing long-term partnerships with those that remain. The result of not assuming a partnership role and focusing on quality is evident in the *BusinessWeek* article quoting Joseph M. Juran (in 1982):

> The automakers turn the screws to the point where it's almost impossible to make money selling to the auto companies. So the vendors have to make it on spare parts in the aftermarket. That gives them a vested interest in failures, a miserable arrangement.

This arrangement has since changed, and the quality of American cars has increased dramatically since that time.

Viewing vendors as partners, rather than as adversaries leads to the ability to implement successfully such cost-saving measures as just-in-time, whereby materials arrive as needed for the production line—eliminating inventory almost entirely. Vendors must be qualified and have policies compatible with your statistical process control and production program. This means moving away from the "low bidder" concept to one that builds long-term relationships. This means developing supplier certification processes. These may vary from commodity to commodity, and may require modifying as process variance is reduced. This also means that some suppliers need to be educated. Some companies find that it is to their advantage to educate their own suppliers.

Figure 3-9 outlines some criteria for vendor selection. Supplier certification is a field of growing interest and has yet to see any major industry-wide standards emerge. If you have a supplier certification program, be sure to include training, or arrange to have low-cost training provided. Otherwise, you may be slighting a superb vendor who is new, or who is completely unfamiliar with Quality Management tools and techniques.

Integrate the Customer into Development

Taking the requirements definition further involves reducing change proposals late in the development life cycle, and in reducing the time from concept

FIGURE 3-9
Vendor Selection Criteria

1. Quality
2. Delivery
3. Performance history
4. Warranties and claim policies
5. Production facilities
6. Price
7. Technical capability
8. Financial position
9. Communication system
10. Reputation
11. Desire for business
12. Management and organization
13. Operating controls
14. Repair service
15. Attitude
16. Impression
17. Packaging
18. Labor relations
19. Geographical location

to showroom floor. American industry still requires many years to reach the showroom floor. Many Japanese companies talk about development times of months, not years. To reduce development time requires linking the voice of the customer with barrier removal, training, empowering the worker, and continuous improvement. In other words, improving requirements definitions may dramatically improve the process, but implementing the other foundational considerations are important to become and remain competitive. A key tool in achieving this reduced development time, and integrating the customer into the development process, is quality function deployment, discussed in Chapter 17.

Concurrent engineering is an emerging multidisciplinary approach to reducing development time dramatically. It seeks to remove disciplinary boundaries and make a "without walls" engineering approach to new product development.

7. EMPOWERING THE WORKER

Empowering the employee means enabling a worker to achieve his or her highest potential. For most American companies, this is new, and may be the most powerful and useful concept in Quality Management. Allowing and facilitating workers to achieve their highest potential may seem obvious or impossible, but it is in fact neither. Empowerment requires turning the organization chart upside down, recognizing that management is in place to aid the worker in overcoming problems they encounter, not to place new roadblocks in the way.

Tapping into optimum individual performance is a holistic endeavor, which most American businesses have been slow to attempt to do. Yet, how can a worker plagued by concerns over a child's day care and older parent's care be devoting all of their energies to their job? The successful company will address and help to adequately resolve these issues.

Empowerment Strategies

Empowering strategies will include:

Ownership. A key strategy in empowering employees is to allow them ownership of a tasking, project, or division. Ownership implies trust and it requires a delegation of authority commensurate with the responsibility of the task. Ownership can also be granted to a team. Ownership also demands that the final resolution of the tasking be in the hands of the owner.

Nitpicking, rearranging, and otherwise finding fault with the tasking upon completion will undermine any attempt at empowerment via ownership.

A simple concept, but hard to do. Just as it is hard for a parent not to correct a child's first attempt at making a bed, putting things away, or cleaning the table. Any correction may ruin weeks of encouragement. Besides, to the child, the bed looks just fine. They've made it to the best of their abilities. If your employees' abilities are none too impressive, it's time to train them.

Value all contributions. Whether or not we appreciate them, it is important to enhance self-esteem of the contributor to accept their contribution and evaluate it. Try it—even if you think it is a goofy idea.

Listen to the least voice. Sometimes the newest and the least have invaluable contributions. It was an upholsterer working on a psychologist's patient's chair who inquired why only the front edge of the chair was worn, which was unusual in the upholsterer's experience. The psychologist deeply pondered the upholsterer's suggestion, and developed the theory of type A personalities.

Everyone has a value. If they didn't why would they be employed? Treat everyone with respect. All work has dignity to it.

Teams must own the problem. Teams are a waste of time if management vetoes or substantially changes their recommendation. Teams must be allowed autonomy. If management is unable to trust the recommendations that come from the team, then management by fear rules, and will spiral to lower and lower productivity.

Give quality awards to customers who have improved their business. Prompt payment to a vendor is their due, not their reward. Reward vendors with exceptional service or greatly improved service by giving them more business, or acknowledging an award in the media.

Delegate authority to the lowest possible organizational level. Constantly ask: Why should I do it? If you've hired competent people, let them do their job. No one knows more about the job than the person directly involved with it. Giving advice on what it was like when you were a neophyte 20 years ago will fall on deaf ears. They will learn how to act within the new environment.

Employee Involvement—A Pleonasm?

A pleonasm is a redundancy in a phrase, such as "large professional football player." If our employees are not involved, who is?[3] Can management alone run the company effectively? Can the union staff? Of course not. Yet millions of dollars are spent every year "motivating" employees, and "involving" employees, or getting them to "participate." The only barriers to worker participation, with rare exception, are those that management has established.

The underlying principle involved in fostering worker participation or empowering is trust. Management must trust its employees. Employees must trust management. Trust is easily erased. One study suggested that a boss was perceived as being negative if she was not complimentary four times more than she was negative. In other words, one "aw shoot" wipes out four "attagirls." Even indirect negative messages come across loudly. Giving an award to one worker may tell the other workers that they didn't perform well. This is why rewards or incentives often fail in a professional setting.

Ironically, promotions can be another way to tell other employees that you don't trust them or that you find them below par. This is due to the large talent pool available. The baby boom has left a large number of competent people plateaued in their career. If the traditional supervisory roles are seen as the leadership track, and these are becoming fewer as organizations become flatter, then crises accompanying promotions are likely to become more common. Those companies that foster growth on the job as a measure of success will retain high-caliber people. Those that maintain strict line orientations as a measure of success will keep experiencing high turnover rates.

Money Is Irrelevant—Almost

Money is becoming less important with the advent of two-income families. Work satisfaction is very important. Few American companies have been able to perceive this and capitalize on it. Money is simply no longer a prime motivator. Maslow's hierarchy (Figure 3–10) provides a look at why this is so. Most professionals have ascended to the Belonging or Esteem stages. Money is a suitable motivator at a lower stage, Safety.

---

[3] An employment ad in a newspaper had as one of its qualifications: "must be able to answer the telephone without being told to do so."

FIGURE 3–10
Maslow's Hierarchy of Needs

Stage	Process	Needs
5th stage	Self-actualization	To achieve one's best.
4th stage	Esteem	To be held in high regard.
3rd stage	Belonging	To be accepted by family and friends.
2nd stage	Safety	To have economic and physical security.
1st stage	Physiological	To eat, sleep, and have shelter.

This is not to say that workers are beginning to refuse raises, but that many other motivators exist other than money, as long as there is enough money to maintain a lifestyle suitable to the Safety stage. Motivation is discussed at length in Chapter 14.

8. TRAINING

Each year, about $210 billion is spent on corporate education, and $230 billion is spent on education from kindergarten through the doctorate level. This training can have a high payoff: Harris Corporation used training to reduce work-in-process inventory by 60 percent, and reduced cost of quality 15 percent. This demonstrates what the president of Harvard, Derek Bok, meant when he said "If you think education is expensive, try ignorance." If spent properly, training can return the investment many times.

The outcome of training is modified behavior. It may be enhanced interpersonal skills or a specific manual skill, but there is a direct, identifiable modification. Training need not consist solely of traditional classroom instruction. Dedicating time to learn how to use a software package could be considered training, especially if the trainee could stop external interruptions, as in a classroom environment. Employees can train other employees very effectively. Erwin Schroedinger, an eminent physicist, once said that the best way for him to learn anything was to have to teach it.

Training someone forces the instructor to consider the task from a different viewpoint. However, to conduct all training by fellow employees or even in-house can cause a stagnation effect. Conferences and seminars are especially good to refresh workers and overcome blindsightedness. Many seminars and courses are conducted at community colleges or local colleges, and are inexpensive. Don't overlook trainers in your own company. Anyone who is unafraid of talking to groups has the potential to train or facilitate training. Training should not be meted out as a punishment or reward. All employees need and deserve training. Training needs and results should be evaluated with the employee to gain insight. Of course, there will be, at times, resistance to certain specific training. It is then useful to send one or a few employees to the training. If the training is successful, the changed behavior will be apparent to fellow workers, and will help convince the skeptical employees of the utility of this training.

Education

Unlike training, education has no such immediately identifiable outcome. The utility of education may not be discoverable for a long period of time, if ever. However, education is vital in promoting a divergent look at the way things are done. Training focuses primarily on the event at hand, thus filling in empty or fuzzy spots on an information matrix (or puzzle). Education may lead us to determine that we are working the wrong puzzle. For example, at a candlemaking factory around the turn of the century, the convergent thinking worker would have considered quality improvements such as making the candle drip less, last longer, and burn more smoothly. The divergent thinker might have suggested manufacturing light bulbs as an improvement.

Divergent thinking is necessary for a business to survive in the long term. Some businesses, as well as government agencies, have instituted the idea of a senior level staff member being a new technology specialist and a technology insertion facilitator. While it would be beneficial if line staff would initiate such actions, their duties often preclude the "stare-at-the-wall" time necessary to consider new technology implementation.

A SAMPLE CURRICULUM

Figure 3–11 shows a sample curriculum. A companywide curriculum should be developed that addresses needs of individual departments. To train everyone, it may well pay to provide a Train the Trainer course to prepare peers to teach some of the courses. Courses should be just long enough to be effective. Anything over three or four days is unlikely to immediately be absorbed into daily work habits. Immediate reinforcement of the training is necessary for it to be effective. After a course in brainstorming, students should have a need to conduct or participate in such a session within two weeks of the training.

THE OMNIPRESENT QUESTION

Quality Management is quite complex. Unfortunately it is difficult to recall all the scores of principles and techniques without referring to a text. Yet it

FIGURE 3-11
Sample TQM Curriculum

First 1-2 Years:
TQM at XYZ Company.
Continuous improvement.
Human behavior in organizations.
Team development.
Problem solving.
Statistical measures.
Organizational communications.
Specific tools training:
  Brainstorming.
  Quality function deployment.
  Cause-effect diagrams.
  Pareto analysis.
  Etc.

Years 2-5:
  Advanced team building.
  Advanced problem solving.
  Specific tools training (continued).

After 5 Years—Ongoing Training:
  Team skills workshops.
  Problem solving seminar.
  Communications workshop.
  Quality improvement seminar.
  Human behavior workshop.

is still pleasant to have a phrase that will serve us like a Swiss Army knife—easy to remember, yet useful for almost any of the situations we encounter. For Quality Management advocates, this phrase is: *What Is the value added?*

This can be the omnipresent question with which we prune old bureaucracies, work rules, and product designs. It does not demand a complex answer, requiring consultants and reports and spreadsheets. The answer does not have to be numeric or measurable in a traditional sense. This question gives us insight into continuous improvement while maintaining a return on investment strategy.

BIBLIOGRAPHY

American Productivity Center. *Allen-Bradley: First Line Supervisors Play Pivotal Role in Employee Communication Program Aimed at Boosting Productivity.* Case study no. 49. Houston, Tex.: American Productivity Center, 1985.

Aubrey, Charles A. II, and Patricia Felkins. *Teamwork: Involving People in Quality and Productivity Improvement.* Milwaukee, Wis.: ASQC Press, 1988.

Baumgarten, S., and J. S. Hensel. "Add Value to Your Service," ed. C. Surprenant. Chicago: *American Marketing Association*, 1987, pp. 105–10.

Booher, Diane. "Quality or Quantity Communication." *Quality Progress* 21, no. 6 (June 1988), pp. 65–68.

Bossert, James L., ed. *Procurement Quality Control.* 4th ed., Milwaukee, Wis.: ASQC Quality Press, 1988.

Ertel, Danny. "How to Design a Conflict Management Procedure That Fits Your Dispute." *Sloan Management Review* 32, no. 4 (Summer 1991), pp. 29–42.

Imai, Masaaki. *Kaizen: The Key to Japan's Competitive Success.* New York: Random House, 1986.

Kaplan, Robert S. "Measuring Manufacturing Performance: A New Challenge for Managerial Accounting Research." *The Accounting Review,* February 1985.

Kiechel, Walter. "Visionary Leadership and Beyond." *Fortune,* July 21, 1986, pp. 127–28.

Kurokawa, Kaneyuki. "Quality and Innovation." *IEEE Circuits and Devices,* July 1988, pp. 3–8.

Lammermeyr, Horst U. *Human Relations—The Key to Quality.* Milwaukee, Wis.: ASQC Quality Press, 1990.

Liswood, Laura A. *Serving Them Right: Innovative and Powerful Customer Retention Strategies.* Milwaukee, Wis.: ASQC Quality Press, 1990.

Luthans, Fred. *Organizational Behavior.* New York: McGraw-Hill, 1973.

Maass, Richard A.; John O. Brown; and James L. Bossert. *Supplier Certification—A Continuous Improvement Strategy,* Milwaukee, Wis.: ASQC Quality Press, 1990.

Main, Jeremy. "Detroit Is Trying Harder for Quality." *BusinessWeek,* November 1, 1982.

Maslow, Abraham H. *Motivation and Personality.* New York: Harper & Row, 1954.

Massey, C. "What You Are Now Is What You Were When." Videotape.

McGregor, Douglas. *Leadership and Motivation.* Cambridge, Mass.: MIT Press, 1983.

Motiska, Paul J., and Karl A. Schilliff. "10 Precepts of Quality." *Quality Progress,* 23, no. 2 (February 1990), pp. 27–28.

Newman, R. G. "Insuring Quality: Purchasing's Role." *Journal of Purchasing and Materials Management,* 1988, pp. 14–20.

Newman, R. G. "The Buyer-Supplier Relationship under Just-in-Time." *Production and Inventory Management Journal,* 1988, pp. 45–50.

Oakland, John S., and Ric Grayson. "Quality Assurance Education and Training in the U.K." *Quality and Reliability Engineering International* 3 (1987), pp. 169–75.

Rout, L. "Hyatt Hotel's Gripe Sessions Help Chief Maintain Communication with Workers." *The Wall Street Journal* 27 (July 16, 1981).

Sandholm, L. "Management Training—A Prerequisite of TQC," *EOQC* 23, no. 4 (December 1989), pp. 5–10.

Scholtes, Peter R., and Heero Hacquebord. "Beginning the Quality Transformation, Part I; and Six Strategies for Beginning the Quality Transformation, Part II." *Quality Progress,* July/August 1988.

Schultz, Louis E. "Creating a Vision for Strategy and Quality: A Way to Help Management Assume Leadership." *Concepts in Quality Proceedings,* November 1988.

Schultz, Louis E. *Pathway to Continuous Improvement.* Bloomington, Minn.: Process Management Institute.

Sink, S. Scott and Thomas C. Tuttle. *Planning and Measurement in Your Organization of the Future.* Atlanta, Ga.: IIE Press, 1991.

Sloan, David, and Scott Weiss. *Supplier Improvement Process Handbook,* ASQC, 1987.

Snee, Ronald D. "Statistical Thinking and Its Contribution to Total Quality." *The American Statistician,* May 1990.

Squires, Frank H. "Who Is Responsible for Quality?," *Quality,* December 1987, p. 73.

Staveley, J. C., and B. G. Dale. "Some Factors to Consider in Developing a Quality-Related Feedback System." *Quality and Reliability Engineering International* 3, no. 4 (1987), pp. 265–71.

Tichy, Noel M., and Mary Anne Devanna. *The Transformational Leader.* New York: John Wiley & Sons, 1986.

Vroom, V. *Work and Motivation.* New York: John Wiley & Sons, 1964.

Zaremba, Alan. *Management in a New Key: Communication in the Modern Organization.* Atlanta, Ga.: IIE Press, 1991.

Zeithaml, Valerie A.; L. L. Berry; and A. Parasuraman. "Communication and Control Processes in the Delivery of Service Quality." *Journal of Marketing* 52 (April 1988), pp. 35–48.

CHAPTER 4

IMPLEMENTATION

Even if you're on the right track, you'll get run over if you just sit there.

Will Rogers

INTRODUCTION

The philosophies, practices, tools, methods, and techniques must be integrated into a coherent implementation plan. There are perhaps as many implementation schemes as there are Quality Management practitioners. The reason for this lies in the individual needs of the organization. Some desire to achieve companywide quality control within a short time frame, others wish to experiment with various techniques and refine them before integrating them throughout the company.

Doing something is not the same thing as doing it well. In the case of Quality Management, not doing it well may be worse than doing nothing, as it sullies the reputation of a fine approach to management. It is difficult to implement Quality Management because it is complex, and because it is very difficult to change attitudes formed over years. Quality Management evolved from the management of quality control, and to many, TQM concepts must include a very heavy dosage of statistical tools. This is a narrow vision of Quality Management, which is attempting to improve the quality of management as well as the product or service. Tools are needed, but they are sterile if not coupled with dynamic management involvement. The tools can be learned over the course of a few days or weeks. Changing a culture of status quo will take months, if not years. The larger the organization, the longer it will take to change.

TQM often espouses a top-down commitment. Top-level managers become enlightened, and then pass the lamp of wisdom onward. Nice theory, but few of us are CEOs or business owners or otherwise at the top of the pyramid. Fortunately, it is not true that Quality Management *must* come from the top—it is the ideal, but not a requirement. Each of us can institute Quality Management on whatever sphere of influence we have. As our success increases, so will interest in exporting Quality Management to other areas of the organization.

This bottom-up approach may not be as awkward as it seems. After all, how can the work force change unless it is either already willing, or encounters a significant or enabling event brought about by top management? If the work force is willing, but was unaware of how to proceed, Quality Management can quickly revolutionize the way work is done. If the work force is not willing, coaching the work force has a slim chance of working. A significant event, such as laying off 25 percent of the work force, may be necessary.

However Quality Management evolves, it is instructive to have some sort of implementation model. There are simply too many tools and concepts to implement to proceed with all of it at once. There are many implementation models. The one presented here is one that is based upon the author's observation of Quality Management principles in action. No magic is involved in picking a model. Adapt one for your unique set of circumstances.

PROCESS

1. Develop a compelling vision. Leaders must have a compelling reason that will sustain them and the company for years to come. Thomas Berry describes Quality Management as a journey, not a destination. Quality Management is not another program. TQM is not an office or a department. Quality Management is a way of organizational life. It is a revolutionary way to invert the organizational hierarchy, put customers first, eliminate managerial deadwood, and overcome whatever stands in the way of fulfilling customer needs.

2. Start small. Implementing a companywide Quality Management plan all at once is suicidal. A single division, department, or branch must first serve as a test site. In this stage vision leadership is articulated and implemented. Try to transform the test site completely before transporting the plan companywide. This means at least 12 to 18 months, and encountering and surmounting at least one crisis.

Don't pick a certain set of members within the test site. Pick everyone in an easily identifiable group, or pick another group. Quality Management will have to work on all employees, not just the best or the worst. Use the PDCA (Plan-Do-Check-Act) cycle (Chapter 17) at all times. Constantly communicate and provide feedback.

Pursue the right way, not the quick way. Visit a Baldrige Award winner. Take courses on the Malcolm Baldrige National Quality Award and benchmarking (see Chapter 18). Read every relevant case study available.

3. Become obsessed. Plan strategically. Become obsessed with implementing the vision. Sweat out the details. These are what the customer sees, not wondrous corporate platitudes. Make abundantly clear that the customer is welcome. This ranges from making the bathrooms spotless to friendly and helpful staff to producing an item or service of world-class quality that the customer will be proud to own and find a pleasure to use. Obsession is imbued from top management. Employees must know who the top managers are—personally. They cannot remain faceless.

4. Celebrate success. Show how well the test site did by making a video, conduct tours of the test site, and allow test site employees to host discussion groups. Rewards are nice, but take it easy. Rewards are often monetary in nature, and prove to be poor motivators (especially among knowledge workers), and actually demotivate others. A job well done is its own reward—work can be a fulfilling and rewarding experience when employees are involved and empowered.

5. Export results to the rest of the organization. Taking the Quality Management process organizationwide is a big step, and will require several years to implement. And that's just the beginning. Employees must understand that Quality Management never stops, and that this is not a program or push. It is way of life to be applied with religious zeal.

A SPIRAL MODEL

The spiral model depicted in Figure 4–1 relates the concepts and principles of Quality Management. While most models appear in linear form, the spiral model serves as a reminder that Quality Management implementation needs to be cascaded through the company, and done iteratively. From the center of the spiral emanates the vision of the organization. The first layer consists of the foundational principles, the second the management dynamics required by midlevel managers and supervisors, and the third layer, or the implementation layer, contains some suggested tool kits. There are three shell layers:

- Vision leaders—top management.
- Vision articulators—middle and supervisory management.
- Vision implementors—supervisors and individuals.

There are four slices that correspond to the four key principles of Quality Management:

- Vision.
- Empowerment.

50 Part 1 Foundational Issues

FIGURE 4–1
Spiral Quality Management Model

[Figure 4–1: Spiral Quality Management Model — concentric spiral diagram with labels including Customer orientation, Continuous improvement tool kit, Motivation, Change management, Culture, Guiding vision, Planning, Leadership, Performance management, Team-building, Evaluation tool kit, Continuous evaluation, Empowerment tool kit, Empowerment, Commitment, Vision tool kit, Vision]

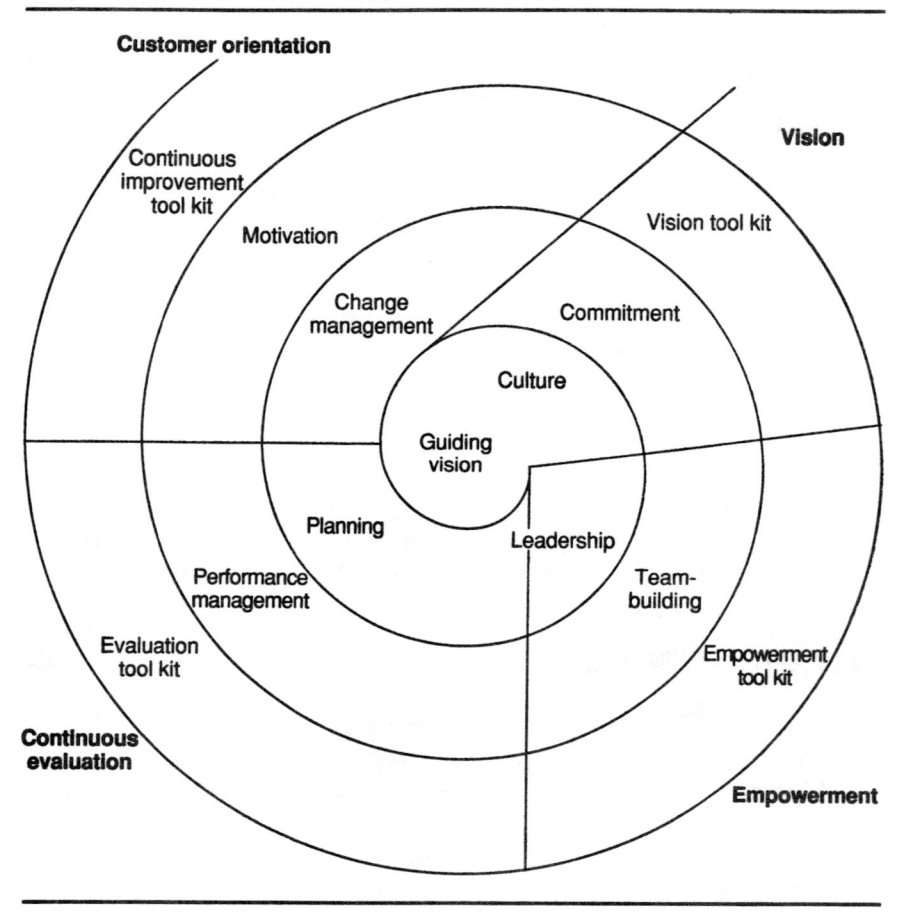

- Continuous evaluation.
- Customer orientation.

Some suggested tools are listed in Figure 4–2. The model is generic enough to be adapted by any organization, and be made specific quite readily.

IMPLEMENTATION ISSUES AND TRAPS

Management must not react to problems with a "How the hell did that happen?," but with a helping attitude. After all, shouldn't the job of man-

FIGURE 4-2
Spiral Model Outline

Vision
Leader task:
  Vision and culture definition
Articulator task:
  Employee involvement
Implementor tool kit:
  Benchmarking
  Force field analysis
  Goal setting
  Systematic diagram

Empowerment
Leader focus:
  Leadership
Articulator task:
  Team building
Implementor tool kit:
  Auditing
  BrainStorming
  Cause-effect diagrams
  Creativity
  Data collection
  Nominal group technique
  Pareto analysis
  Process decision program chart
  Quality circles
  Service quality
  Time management
  Work flow analysis

Continuous Evaluation
Leader focus:
  Strategic planning
Articulator task:
  Performance management
Implementor tool kit:
  Auditing
  Benchmarking
  BrainStorming
  Cause-effect diagrams
  Control charts
  Data collection
  Delphi technique
  Design of experiments
  Evolutionary operation
  Failure modes, effects, and
    criticality analysis (FMECA)
  Flowcharts
  Nominal group technique
  Quality costs
  Sampling
  Statistical measures
  Five Ws, one Y

Customer Orientation
Leader focus:
  Change management
Articulator task:
  Motivation
Implementor tool kit:
  Benchmarking
  Data collection
  Delphi technique
  Foolproofing
  Quality function deployment
  Service quality
  Nominal group techniques
  Quality function deployment
  Sampling

agement be to help with exceptions to the routine? If things always worked smoothly, with no unusual circumstances or problems, why bother with managers?

Douglas Patterson points out a number of traps to avoid when implementing Quality Management:

Delegating Quality Management authority. Quality Management must be the responsibility of top management—first. Then it must become everyone's responsibility. As Deming, Juran, and others point out, the management culture must change in order for Quality Management to be properly instituted.

Quality Management is a new name for existing programs. Statistical process control, analysis of variance, quality circles, cross-functional teams are all part of Quality Management, but do not constitute it in its entirety. Quality Management requires a vision and principles, as well as tools.

Do it right the first time. Too vigorous and literal an implementation of this concept will stifle creativity. Failures are more than OK; they are opportunities for learning.

Quality Management is statistical quality control and quality circles. Tools are only a part of the picture. Humanistic management principles, discussed in Part 3, Management Dynamics, and the principles discussed in this section are necessary for achieving the goals of Quality Management.

Barry Sheehy has developed some guidelines on surviving the inevitable: the first crisis of the Quality Management or quality improvement program:

1. Acknowledge the crisis.
2. Consider it a hidden opportunity.
3. Make sure everyone understands that there is no going back.
4. Give voice to your fears/concerns—but don't back down in the face of naysayers.
5. Recall accomplishments that have occurred so far.
6. Get counsel from workers and suppliers, not your fears.
7. Ask for advice. No voice is too small.
8. Revise your plan and inform everyone of the changes.

Sheehy also recommends the following preventative or mitigating factors:

1. Build backsliding/setbacks into your plan.
2. Underpromise and overdeliver.

3. Plan a renewal at about month 12.
4. Review goals for their attainability.
5. Record all accomplishments.

While a crisis is unavoidable, preparing for it can considerably lessen the damage to the credibility of the program.

BIBLIOGRAPHY

All of the following are highly recommended. Thomas Berry's work is particularly engaging.

Berry, Thomas H. *Managing the Total Quality Transformation.* New York: McGraw-Hill, 1990.

Docstader, S. L. "Managing TQM Implementations: A Matrix Approach." Unpublished manuscript. San Diego: Navy Personnel Research & Development Center, 1987.

Hunt, Daniel V. *Quality in America: How to Implement a Competitive Quality Program.* Homewood, Ill.: Richard D. Irwin, 1991.

Mansir, Brian E., and Nicholas R. Schacht. *Total Quality Management: A Guide to Implementation,* Bethesda, Md., 1989.

Patterson, Douglas O. "Saying Is One Thing, Doing Is Another!" *Journal of the Institute of Environmental Sciences,* January/February 1991, pp. 17–20.

Scholtes, Peter R., and Heero Harquebord. "Six Strategies for Beginning the Quality Transformation, Part II." *Quality Progress,* August 1988.

Sheehy, Barry. "Hitting the Wall: How to Survive Your Quality Program's First Crisis." *National Productivity Review,* 9, no. 3 (Summer 1990), pp. 329–35.

U.S. Department of Defense. *TQM Implementation Guide, Volumes I and II.* U.S. GPO, February 1990.

Weaver, Charles N. *TQM: A Step-by-Step Guide to Implementation.* Milwaukee, Wis.: ASQC Quality Press, 1991.

PART 2

QUALITY MASTERS

5. PHILIP B. CROSBY
6. W. EDWARDS DEMING
7. ARMAND V. FEIGENBAUM
8. KAORU ISHIKAWA
9. JOSEPH M. JURAN
10. TOM PETERS
11. GENICHI TAGUCHI
12. HISTORICAL MASTERS

INTRODUCTION

Charismatic pacesetters such as Deming, Juran, or Crosby are often identified (or even equated) with the Quality Management movement. Their magnetism has resulted in passionate devotees and "disciples" of the various masters, each proclaiming their pundit to have revealed the one true path to total quality enlightenment. The squabbling that occasionally occurs between each guru's camp sometimes resembles religious "heresy" disputes, where much arguing proceeds over differences without distinction. Because their writings are motivational, it is important to read and reflect upon more than one of the masters prior to embarking on a total Quality Management program. While all of their platforms agree to within 95 percent, that last 5 percent difference may be appealing.

Because most of the masters have written several volumes on their thoughts on TQM, it is useful to have a condensed version of their major tenets readily available. Of course, in the space available it is impossible to convey all of the profound notions contained in these volumes, or to do justice to the subtlety of many of their points. However, it should aid in understanding the differences and similarities of their respective approaches—just as you wouldn't mistake a field guide description for a tree, so this section should not be mistaken as an exhaustive catalog of a master's canon. Presented in this section are thumbnail sketches of the quality masters and their primary teachings, punctuated with some of their words of wisdom. The reader is strongly encouraged to read the major works of the quality masters described. An essential bibliography is provided in Part 5, Resources. While some may seem bulky (*Thriving on Chaos* by Tom Peters runs more than 700 pages in paperback; Feigenbaum's magnum opus *Total Quality Control* runs over 800), they can be read very quickly, and are worth reading several times.

Why this particular set of seven leaders? These seven are the most popular and are commonly identified with the Quality Management effort today. There are many other masters in the quality field, such as Shigeo Shingo, Shewhart, Dodge, A. J. Duncan, Mizuno, Ohno, Godfrey, Martin Smith, Scherkenbach, and others who advance and encourage the state of the art of quality management techniques. Others may be gleaned from the quality-related service directory listed annually in the August issue of *Quality Progress*. Many of these experts offer training and consulting, and may be far more accessible, while as illuminating, as the masters profiled here. Space limits force consideration of a small number of leaders, and this set has succeeded in appealing to an unusually large audience, often far outside the traditional bailiwick of quality control specialists. Yet these masters are closely identified with quality management per se, rather than any and all aspects of management; otherwise Peter Drucker would figure prominently here. His influence on management has been extraordinary, and will reach well into the next millennium. No Quality Management library should be without his works, and he is frequently referred to in this book.

A QUICK FIELD GUIDE

Crosby is closely associated with the zero defects concept, but in later years has shifted more toward the mainstream of Quality Management thinking. Deming is a godlike figure of quality, and his "14 Points" pop up everywhere. Feigenbaum's fairly early work on total quality control is well worth reading; he has fallen out of the limelight somewhat as he does not seem to seek publicity. Ishikawa was the aristocrat of Japanese quality, and is associated with his "Seven Tools." Juran is an indefatigable promoter of Quality Management, and is famous for his indispensable *Quality Control Handbook*. Peters is an annalist of business excellence, taking an empirical and anecdotal approach. Taguchi focused narrowly on design of experiments, but his influence in Japan has been dramatic, and his work may present the "next phase" beyond statistical quality control.

Deming and Peters are the most revolutionary, demanding a managerial transformation. Crosby and Feigenbaum see quality fitting in more as a quality promotion department that acts as a facilitator/consultant. Ishikawa works within an existing organizational framework, but his ideas benefit from Japan's historically better access to top management. Lately, Juran has also called for a revolution.

Most quality masters have the context of the medium to large organizations in mind. However, almost all masters' tenets can be applied to small businesses as well. In fact, especially when one reads Peters's works, it would seem that the intent is to achieve integrated small business units within one corporation. Many of the human aspects of the tenets are readily achievable in small businesses. Small businesses have the ability to transform themselves quickly. Their disadvantage can be a lack of resources, both human and capital.

Which master is for your organization depends upon the corporate culture (Chapter 13) and the level of top-managerial commitment. Assiduously following any one of them would lead to a total quality transformation. There is no *best* master, although Deming is highly favored by many, and provides a comprehensive philosophy, which is essential to Quality Management implementation.

IMPLEMENTING A MASTER'S STRATEGY

It is becoming apparent that while it would be nice to perform a transition into Quality Management, what is really needed is the phoenixlike transformation of Peters or Deming. Like a sports coach, Quality Management masters offer a package, and must be dealt with whole, not in pieces. While you may be able to synthesize your own game plan from the coaches here, be wary of "cafeteria management"—taking only those aspects that appeal to you from each master. If there is something unpalatable in their dicta (such as giving up management parking spots), this may expose a management weakness (such as perpetuating an Us-versus-Them management to employee climate) that needs to be corrected, and may actually be crucial to successfully executing the plan in your organization. Partial implementation is often a mistake. View it as if you had built a race car without an engine. While it may look nice, it'll never cross the finish line.

A more common mistake made in implementing a Quality Management approach is to espouse it loudly from the top, somehow expecting everyone to become wildly motivated by meetings that may look the same as always, and memos that, while more enthusiastic, still lack specifics. Employees

many, and various roadblocks and pitfalls have been identified throughout this book. Change cannot come without mistakes along the way.

Quality Management is definitely not a fad, having been around in some form for 50 years, or, if we may challenge the reader's belief, some 2,500 years (see Chapter 12, Historical Masters). This is because Quality Management is not driven by present economic forces, but founded on such questions as: What is human nature? How must we manage? What is the simplest, yet most powerful tool I can find?

Situational economics has created trendy management guides such as *The Peter Principle* and *Leadership Secrets of Attila the Hun*. Quality Management also transcends single personal experiences, such as *Swim with the Sharks*. These works do not provide us with a permanent foundation on which to build management skills, but they make for enjoyable reading, and indeed, can even help us understand the times in which they were created and provide valuable personal and managerial insight. For example the Peter principle presents an interesting thesis for the U.S. manufacturing capability erosion of the 1950s and 1960s. Today however, in the face of massive layoffs of skilled managers and a highly talented pool of professionals in the unemployment line, his thesis seems cruel and untrue. Peter Drucker provides a reflective and cogent discussion of today's condition in his work *The New Realities*. Lloyd Dobyns and Clare Crawford-Mason also provide an intriguing look at the present global market in their work *Quality or Else*.

BIBLIOGRAPHY

Blanchard, Kenneth, and Spencer Johnson. *The One Minute Manager.* ed. Pat Golbitz. New York: William Morrow, 1982.

DeYoung, H. Garrett. "Preachings of Quality Gurus: Do It Right the First Time." *Electronic Business,* October 16, 1989, pp. 88–94.

Dobyns, Lloyd, and Clare Crawford-Mason. *Quality or Else.* Boston: Houghton Mifflin, 1991.

Drucker, Peter. *The New Realities.* New York: Harper & Row, 1989.

Lodge, Charles. "Six Gurus Show the Way to Improved Product Quality." *Plastics World,* August 1989, pp. 29–40.

Main, Jeremy. "Under the Spell of Quality Gurus." *Fortune,* August 18, 1986, pp. 30–34.

McKay, Harvey. *Swim with the Sharks.* New York: William Morrow, 1988.

Peter, Laurence J., and Raymond Hull. *The Peter Principle: Why Things Always Go Wrong.* New York: William Morrow, 1969.

Roberts, Wess. *Leadership Secrets of Attila the Hun.* New York: Warner Books, 1989.

Wood, Robert Chapman. "The Prophets of Quality." *Quality Review* 2, no. 4 (Winter 1988), pp. 18–25.

CHAPTER 5

PHILIP B. CROSBY*

BRIEF BIOGRAPHY

Philip B. Crosby was born in 1926 in Wheeling, West Virginia. Crosby has a degree in podiatry (his father's profession) but decided he didn't like it. In 1952 he became a reliability engineer for Crosley Corporation in Richmond, Indiana. He later worked for the Martin Corporation from 1957 to 1965. Crosby was in charge of quality on the Pershing missile project. From 1965 to 1979 he was the director (vice president status) of quality for ITT. In 1979, he founded Philip Crosby Associates (PCA) in Winter Park, Florida. In 1991 he retired from PCA and began Career IV, Inc. to help grow executives.

MAJOR TENETS

Philip B. Crosby is most closely associated with the idea of zero defects which he created in 1961. To Crosby, quality is conformance to requirements, which is measured by the cost of nonconformance. Poor or high quality has no meaning, only nonconformance and conformance. Using this approach means that one arrives at a performance goal of zero defects.

Crosby equates quality management with prevention. Therefore, inspection, testing, checking, and other nonpreventive techniques have no place. Statistical levels of compliance program people for failure. Crosby maintains that there is absolutely no reason for having errors or defects in any product or service.

Companies should adopt a quality "vaccine" to prevent nonconformance. The three ingredients of this vaccine are: determination, education,

---

*The authors would like to thank Dr. Crosby for his review and comments on this chapter.

and implementation. Quality improvement is a process, not a program; it should be permanent and lasting.

Supplier quality audits are nearly useless, unless the vendor is totally incompetent. It is impossible to know if the supplier's quality system will provide the required quality merely by auditing their plan.

Zero defects is not a slogan. It is a management performance standard. Further demotivating employees by constant exhortation is not the answer. Crosby believes that in the 1960s various Japanese companies properly applied zero defects, using it as an engineering tool, with responsibility of proper implementation left to management. By contrast, zero defects was used as a motivational tool in the United States, with responsibility left to the worker, where it failed. This strategy requires management commitment and technical direction. Crosby's 14 steps to quality improvement and his four absolutes are provided below (from *Quality Is Free* and *The Eternally Successful Organization*).

CROSBY'S 14 STEPS TO QUALITY IMPROVEMENT

1. Make it clear that management is committed to quality.
2. Form quality improvement teams with representatives from each department.
3. Determine how to measure where current and potential quality problems lie.
4. Evaluate the cost of quality and explain its use as a management tool.
5. Raise the quality awareness and personal concern of all employees.
6. Take formal actions to correct problems identified through previous steps.
7. Establish a committee for the zero defects program.
8. Train all employees to actively carry out their part of the quality improvement program.
9. Hold a "zero defects day" to let all employees realize that there has been a change.
10. Encourage individuals to establish improvement goals for themselves and their groups.
11. Encourage employees to communicate to management the obstacles they face in attaining their improvement goals.
12. Recognize and appreciate those who participate.

13. Establish quality councils to communicate on a regular basis.
14. Do it all over again to emphasize that the quality improvement program never ends.

ABSOLUTES OF QUALITY MANAGEMENT

- Quality means conformance to requirements. If you intend to do it right the first time, everyone must know what *it* is.
- Quality comes from prevention. Vaccination is the way to prevent organizational disease. Prevention comes from training, discipline, example, leadership, and more.
- Quality performance standard is zero defects (or defect-free). Errors should not be tolerated. Errors are not tolerated in financial management; why should they be in manufacturing?
- Quality measurement is the price of nonconformance.

BIBLIOGRAPHY

Crosby, Philip B. *Quality Is Free*. New York: McGraw-Hill, 1979.
Crosby, Philip B. *Quality without Tears*. New York: McGraw-Hill, 1984.
Crosby, Philip B. "Quality—Management's Choice." *Quality,* Anniversary Issue, 1987.
Crosby, Philip B. *The Eternally Successful Organization*. New York: McGraw-Hill, 1988.

CHAPTER 6

W. EDWARDS DEMING

BRIEF BIOGRAPHY

W. Edwards Deming was born on October 14, 1900 in Sioux City, Iowa. Shortly thereafter, his family moved to Powell, Wyoming. Deming graduated with a B.S. in physics from the University of Wyoming in 1921, and graduated from Yale with a Ph.D. in mathematical physics in 1928. He worked for the U.S. Census Bureau during and after World War II. In 1950, Deming went to Japan to help conduct a population census, and lectured to top business leaders on statistical quality control. Deming told the Japanese they could become world-class quality leaders if they followed his advice. During the 1950s, Deming again traveled to Japan at the behest of the Japanese Union of Scientists and Engineers (JUSE). Because of his refusal of payment for his lectures (Japan at the time was quite impoverished), JUSE used the funds to establish the Deming Prize, which is the most honored quality award in Japan today. In the 1980 NBC White Paper, "If Japan Can, Why Can't We," he was called the "founder of the third wave of the Industrial Revolution." Today Deming is generally regarded as the top leader in quality management, and is still cited as the founder of the third wave of the Industrial Revolution (the first wave occurred in the early 19th century with simple automation; the second wave occurred with assembly concepts in the late 19th century, and the third wave is occurring with the information/computer revolution).

BASIC TENETS

Quality does not mean luxury. Quality is a predictable degree of uniformity and dependability, at low cost, suited to the market. In other words, quality is whatever the customer needs and wants. And since the customer's needs and desires are always changing, the solution to defining quality in terms of the customer is to redefine requirements constantly.

Productivity improves as variability decreases. Since all things vary, quality control is needed. Statistical control does not imply absence of defect goals and services, but rather, it allows prediction of the limits of variations. There are two types of variation: chance and assignable. It is futile to attempt to eradicate defects caused by chance. However, it can be very difficult to distinguish between the two, or to determine assignable causes. It is not enough to meet specifications; one has to reduce variation as well.

Deming is extremely critical of U.S. management and is an advocate of worker participation in decision making. He claims that management is responsible for 94 percent of quality problems, and points out that it is management's task to help people work smarter, not harder. Deming insists that one of the first steps is for management to remove the barriers that rob the workers of their right to do a good job. Motivational programs which offer lip service have no place here; workers distinguish between sloganeering and commitment.

Inspection of incoming or outgoing goods is too late, ineffective, and costly. Inspection neither improves quality, nor guarantees it. Additionally, inspection usually allows a certain number of defects. The best recognition one can give a quality vendor is to award the vendor more business. Deming advocates sole sourcing, believing that multiple sourcing for protection is a costly practice. The advantages of sole sourcing include better vendor commitment, eliminating small differences between products from two suppliers, and simplifying accounting and paperwork. Counter to the argument that single source can mean paying a higher price, Deming believes that the policy of always trying to drive down the price of purchased items, without regard to quality and service, can drive good vendors and good service out of business.

Deming's celebrated 14 Points, seven deadly diseases, and a number of obstacles are summarized below. They are elaborated at length in Deming's work *Out of the Crisis,* and in several of the works listed in the bibliography, most notably the works by Scherkenbach, Tribus, and Walton.

DEMING'S 14 POINTS

1. Create constancy of purpose for improvement of product and service. An organizational vision must guide the corporate culture and provide a focus to the organization. This vision equips the organization with a long-term perspective. Measure management commitment, and benchmark how the organization is doing relative to other related firms.

2. Adopt the new philosophy. Western management must awaken to the challenge, and assume a new leadership role. The quality revolution is equal in economic import as the Industrial Revolution. It is concurrent with the globalization of the economy.

3. Cease dependence upon inspection to achieve quality. Introduce modern quality tools such as statistical process control, evolutionary operation, design of experiments, and quality function deployment. Inspection only measures a problem, and does not allow any correction of the problem. It is often said that one cannot "inspect in quality."

4. Minimize total cost by working with a single supplier—end the practice of awarding business on the price tag alone. Don't blindly award business to the low bidder. Instead, minimize total cost. Move toward a single supplier for any one item, establishing a long-term relationship of loyalty and trust. Vendor certification programs and total life-cycle cost analysis play a role here.

5. Improve constantly and forever every process. Simply fixing problems is no longer enough. Constantly improve quality and productivity, thus constantly decrease costs. Prevent defects and improve the process. Don't fight fires—this is not quality improvement, it's management by crisis. Improvement requires feedback mechanisms from customers and vendors.

6. Institute training on the job. Training applies to all levels of the organization, from the lowest to the highest. Do not overlook the possibility that the best trainers may be your own employees.

7. Adopt and institute leadership. Leadership emanates from knowledge, expertise, and interpersonal skills, not level of authority. Everyone can and should be a leader. Leadership qualities are no longer mysterious and innate—they can be learned (Chapter 13). Leaders remove barriers that prevent people and machines from achieving the optimum.

8. Drive out fear. Fear stems fom insecure leadership which must rely on work rules, authority, punishment, and a corporate culture based upon internal competition—grading on a curve has no place within a business. It may also come from physical and emotional abuse by peers and superiors. Fear snuffs out creativity, which is the engine for quality improvement. This fear can be defeated by identifying and overcoming gaps in communication, culture, and training. Systemic factors may also promote management by fear, such as performance evaluations, bonus programs, and work quotas.

9. Break down barriers between staff areas. Everyone must work as a team, working toward the good of the team. Teamwork is imperative in modern management. New organizational structures may be needed (Chapter 13). Turning the organizational chart upside down is a frightening experience, but may well be required to achieve the proper balance and perspective.

10. Eliminate slogans, exhortations, and targets for the work force. Programs or campaigns which command a task but leave the worker powerless to achieve the objective constitute management by fear.

11. Eliminate numerical quotas for the work force and numerical goals for management. Eliminate management by objective, or more precisely, management by numbers. Substitute leadership. Numerical quotas disregard statistical notions which impact all workers. Not all workers can be above average; nor can they all be below. Traditional industrial engineering practice is "management by numbers" and this is precisely what Deming is referring to. Work measurement worked well at a certain stage in industrial development, but society and work have evolved beyond that. Today work quotas can impose a quality and production ceiling, rather than a target. Natural variation is ignored in these systems, and the numbers game takes precedence over all other business concerns.

12. Remove barriers that rob people of pride of workmanship. Eliminate the annual rating system. Remove barriers that rob the hourly worker of their pride of workmanship. The responsibility of supervisors must be changed from volume and bottom line to quality. Remove barriers that rob people in management and in engineering of their right to pride of workmanship. This means abolishment of the annual or merit rating and of management by objective.

13. Institute a vigorous program of education and self-improvement for everyone. Training provides an immediate change in behavior. Results of education may not manifest themselves immediately, but it can have far-reaching long-term effects. Self-improvement is an ongoing task of education and self-development. This may mean offering courses in time management, stress reduction, allowing employees work time to do physical activity if they have a sedentary job, allowing employees who have active jobs to partake in mentally challenging tasks or education.

14. Put everybody in the company to work to accomplish the transformation. Top-management commitment is required to put everybody in the company to work to accomplish the transformation. The transformation is everybody's job.

DEMING'S SEVEN DEADLY DISEASES

1. Lack of constancy of purpose. Lack of vision results in a lack of focus and a lack of discipline, which can lead to a deterioration of the job environment and the organization itself.

2. Emphasis on short-term profits; short-term thinking. This is actually saying the same thing as above, but is so common among American businesses that it deserves a separate entry. Amplifying the quarterly report into the be-all and end-all of the business is organizational suicide. Unfortunately there are many institutional mechanisms working against this aspect of the transformation.

3. Annual performance reviews. The effects of performance appraisals are devastating. Management by objective, on a go, no-go basis, is the same thing. Management by fear would be better than these extremely demotivational tools.

4. Mobility of management; job hopping. Little value is placed in Western society on staying in the job for years, and performing at one's peak.

5. Use of visible figures only for management. If information is relevant to their work, they need to be informed.

6. Excessive medical costs. Books on "stress" abound. The reason for this is the intense dissatisfaction in working in the contemporary corporate workplace; a corollary to this is the entrepreneurial boom. Simply put, people who enjoy their work stay healthy (see Chapter 15.1 on Stress Management). Health plans which cover preventive measures must be selected over those that merely react to problems.

7. *Excessive costs of liability.* This is fueled by lawyers that work on contingency fees, in a society that highly values a profession that provides little or no added value.

DEMING'S OBSTACLES

1. Neglect of long-range planning and transformation.
2. The idea that problems are solved with automation, gadgets, and other "things."
3. Partaking of a smorgasbord approach to implementing quality improvements without basic principles will prove disastrous.
4. The attitude that "Our problems are different" leads to ignoring basic principles.
5. The obsolescence in schools (grade school through graduate school) must be overcome.
6. Reliance on quality control departments to "take care of all our problems of quality." Quality must become part of everyone's job.
7. Blaming the work force for problems. There must be improvement of the system as well as a product. Defect free workmanship means nothing if the wrong product is being made.
8. Quality by inspection. Quality cannot be inspected in. Meeting specifications is not quality, either—they don't tell the whole story.
9. False starts can result from mass teaching with little guidance in implementation. Other false starts happen when the idea to be implemented will require years of cultural change. Deming points to the example of Quality Control circles being poorly implemented in the United States due to a lack of understanding and action on the part of management.
10. The unstaffed computer. Computers can take tedium out of calculations, but not the need for interpretation. Expert systems have not advanced to the point of a "Lights Out" factory of robots, and it is quite likely this will not happen for a long time.
11. Inadequate testing. Prototypes are a lot cheaper than a massive production failure. Computer-aided manufacturing allows "soft"

prototypes that are easy to change, and do a fair job at mimicking reality. A "hard" prototype can be built after experimenting with many different soft ones.

12. "Anyone that comes to try to help us must understand all about our business" is an arrogant attitude that leads to failure. Answers can be found within the organization and from outside consultants and other sources.

BIBLIOGRAPHY

Aguayo, Rafael. *Dr. Deming: The American Who Taught the Japanese about Quality.* New York: Fireside Press, 1991.

Baillie, Allan S. "The Deming Approach: Being Better than the Best." *Advanced Management Journal* 51 (Autumn 1986), pp. 15–19.

Butterfield, Ronald W. "Deming's 14 Points Applied to Service." *Training: The Magazine of Human Resources Develop.* 28 (March 1991), pp. 50–56.

Deming, W. Edwards. *Japanese Methods for Productivity and Quality.* Washington, D.C.: George Washington University, 1981.

Deming, W. Edwards. *Quality, Productivity and Competitive Position.* Cambridge, Mass.: Center for Advanced Engineering Study, MIT Press, 1982.

Deming, W. Edwards. "Quality: Management's Commitment to Quality." *Business,* 35 (January 1985), pp. 50–55.

Deming, W. Edwards. *Out of the Crisis.* Cambridge, Mass.: Center for Advanced Engineering Study, MIT Press, 1986.

Deming, W. Edwards. "New Principles of Leadership." *Modern Materials Handling* 42 (October 1987), pp. 37–41.

Deming, W. Edwards. "Out of the Crisis," *Journal of Organizational Behavior Management* 10 (Spring 1989), pp. 205–13.

Duncan, W. Jack, and Joseph G. Van Matre. "The Gospel according to Deming: Is It Really New?" *Business Horizons* 33 (July/August 1990), pp. 3–17.

Gabor, Andrea. *The Man Who Discovered Quality: The Management Genius of W. Edwards Deming.* Milwaukee, Wis.: ASQC Quality Press, 1991.

Gitlow, Howard, and Shelly Gitlow. *The Deming Guide to Quality and Competitive Position.* Englewood Cliffs, N.J.: Prentice-Hall, 1986.

Rosander, A. C. *Deming's 14 Points Applied to Services.* Milwaukee, Wis.: ASQC Quality Press, 1991.

Scherkenbach, William. *The Deming Route to Quality and Productivity: Road Maps and Roadblocks.* Washington, D.C.: CeePress, George Washington University, 1986.

Scholtes, Peter. *An Elaboration of Deming's Teachings on Performance Appraisal.* Madison, Wisconsin: Joiner Associates, Inc., 1987.

Tribus, M. *Deming's Redefinition of Management*. Cambridge, Mass.: Center for Advanced Engineering Study, MIT Press, 1985.

Tribus, M. *Reducing Deming's 14 Points to Practice*. Cambridge, Mass.: Center for Advanced Engineering Study, MIT Press, 1984.

Walton, Mary. *The Deming Management Method*. New York: Putnam, 1986.

Walton, Mary. *Deming Management at Work*. Milwaukee, Wis.: ASQC Quality Press, 1990.

CHAPTER 7

ARMAND V. FEIGENBAUM

BRIEF BIOGRAPHY

Armand Vallin Feigenbaum was born in 1922. In 1944 he was the top quality expert for General Electric in Schenectady, New York. He received a Ph.D. from the Massachusetts Institute of Technology in 1951. While there he authored his magnum opus, *Total Quality Control* (now in its third edition). In 1958 he was made executive of manufacturing operations for General Electric worldwide. In 1968 Feigenbaum founded General Systems in Pittsfield, Massachusetts, where he serves as president.

BASIC TENETS

Feigenbaum championed the phrase *total quality control* in the United States. Total quality control approaches quality as a strategic business tool that requires awareness by everyone in the company, just as cost and schedule are in most companies today. Quality reaches far beyond defect management on the shop floor; it is a philosophy and commitment to excellence.

Quality is a way of corporate life, a way of managing. Total quality control has an organizationwide impact that involves implementation of customer-oriented quality activities. This is a prime responsibility of general management, as well as the mainline operations of marketing, engineering, production, industrial relations, finance, and service, and also of the quality control function itself at the most economical levels. Feigenbaum's definition of total quality control is: Total quality means being excellence-driven, rather than defect-driven.

An overview of Feigenbaum's approach is given in the Three Steps to Quality and The Four Deadly Sins. These and other ideas are explored further in the Nineteen Steps to Quality Improvement, derived from several of Feigenbaum's works.

THREE STEPS TO QUALITY

1. Quality leadership. There must be continuous management emphasis and leadership in quality. Quality must be thoroughly planned in specific terms. This approach is excellence-driven rather than the traditional failure-driven approach. Attaining quality excellence means keeping a constant focus on maintaining quality. This sort of continuous approach is very demanding on management. The establishment of a quality circle program or a corrective action team is not sufficient for its ongoing success.

2. Modern quality technology. The traditional quality department cannot resolve 80 to 90 percent of quality problems. In a modern setting, all members of the organization must be responsible for quality of their product or service. This means integrating office staff into the process, as well as engineers and shopfloor workers. Error-free performance should be the goal. New techniques must be evaluated and implemented as appropriate. What may be an acceptable level of quality to a customer today may not be tomorrow.

3. Organizational commitment. Continuous motivation is required, and more. Training that is specifically related to the task at hand is of paramount importance. Consideration of quality as a strategic element of business planning needs to occur in the United States.

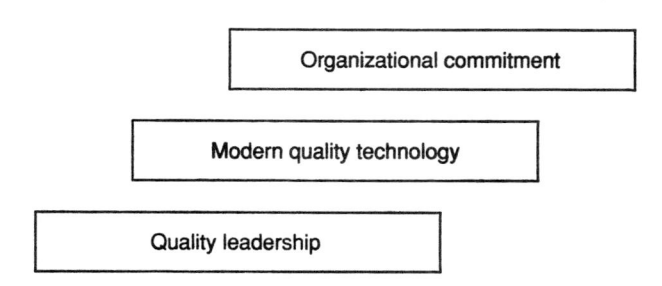

```
            ┌──────────────────────────────┐
            │  Organizational commitment   │
            └──────────────────────────────┘
      ┌──────────────────────────────┐
      │   Modern quality technology  │
      └──────────────────────────────┘
┌──────────────────────────────┐
│      Quality leadership      │
└──────────────────────────────┘
```

FOUR DEADLY SINS

1. Hothouse quality. Quality gets top-level attention in a "fireworks display" manner. These programs disappear from view when production demands become heavy, or something else captures top-level attention.

2. Wishful thinking. The federal government cannot wave a wand and make imports go away, nor should it engage in protectionist activity. This is complacency that will be costly later.

3. Producing overseas. A competitive advantage cannot be gained by having someone else fight our "quality war." The radio, television, auto, and consumer electronics industries have proven this.

4. Confining quality to the factory. Quality achievement is for everyone in every sector of the company.

NINETEEN STEPS TO QUALITY IMPROVEMENT

1. Total quality control defined. TQC may be defined as: An effective system for integrating the quality development, quality maintenance, and quality improvement efforts of the various groups in an organization so as to enable marketing, engineering, production, and service at the most economical levels which allow for full-customer satisfaction.

2. Quality versus quality. "Big Q" or Quality refers to luxurious quality whereas "little q" refers to high quality, not necessarily luxury. Regardless of an organization's niche, little q must be closely maintained and improved.

3. Control. In the phrase "quality control," the word *control* represents a management tool with four steps:
1. Setting quality standards.
2. Appraising conformance to these standards.
3. Acting when the standards are exceeded.
4. Planning for improvements in the standards.

4. Integration. Quality control requires the integration of often uncoordinated activities into a framework. This framework should place the responsibility for customer-driven quality efforts across all activities of the enterprise.

5. Quality increases profits. Total quality control programs are highly cost effective because of their results in improved levels of customer satisfaction, reduced operating losses and field service costs, and improved utilization of resources. Without quality, customers will not return. Without return customers, no business will long survive.

6. Quality is expected, not desired. Quality begets quality. As one supplier becomes quality oriented, other suppliers must meet or exceed this new standard.

7. Humans impact quality. The greatest quality improvements are likely to come from humans improving the process, not adding machines.

8. TQC applies to all products and services. No person or department is exempted from supplying quality services and products to its customer.

9. Quality is a total life-cycle consideration. Quality control enters into all phases of the industrial production process, starting with the customer's specification, through design engineering and assembly to shipment of the product and installation, including field service for a customer who remains satisfied with the product.

10. Controlling the process. These controls fall into four natural classifications: new design control, incoming material control, product control, and special process studies.

11. A total quality system may be defined as. The agreed companywide and plantwide operating work structure, documented in effective, integrated technical and managerial procedures, for guiding the coordinated actions of the people, the machines, and the information of the company and plant in the best and most practical ways to assure customer quality satisfaction and economical costs of quality. The quality system provides integrated and continuous control to all key activities, making it truly organizationwide in scope.

12. Benefits. Benefits often resulting from total quality programs are improvement in product quality and design, reduction in operating costs and losses, improvement in employee morale, and reduction of production-line bottlenecks.

13. Cost of quality. Quality costs are a means for measuring and optimizing total quality control activities. Operating quality costs are divided into four different classifications: prevention costs, appraisal costs, internal failure costs, and external failure costs. These costs are discussed at length in Chapter 18.

14. Organize for quality control. It is necessary to demonstrate that *quality is everybody's job.* Every organizational component has a quality-related responsibility; for example, marketing for determining customers' quality preferences, engineering for specifying product quality specifications, and shop supervision for building quality into the product. Make this responsibility explicit and visible.

15. Quality facilitators, not quality cops. The quality control organization acts as a touchstone for communicating new results in the company, providing new techniques, acting as a facilitator, and in general resembles an internal consultant, rather than a police force of quality inspectors.

16. Continuous commitment. Management must recognize at the outset of its total quality control program that this program is not a temporary quality improvement or quality cost reduction project.

17. Use statistical tools. Statistics are used in an overall quality control program whenever and wherever they may be useful, but statistics are only one part of the total quality control pattern. They are not the pattern itself. The development of advanced electronic and mechanical test equipment has provided order of magnitude improvements to this task.

18. Automation is not a panacea. Automation is complex and can become an implementation nightmare. Be sure the best human-oriented activities are implemented before being convinced that automation is the answer.

19. Control quality at the source. The creator of the product or the deliverer of the service must be able to control the quality of their product or service. Delegate authority, if necessary. Norton Stores has the simple company policy of "Use your own best judgment," and allows its employees the authority and freedom that this policy requires.

BIBLIOGRAPHY

Feigenbaum, Armand V. *Total Quality Control.* 3rd ed. New York: McGraw-Hill, 1983.

Feigenbaum, Armand V. "Total Quality Leadership," *Quality* 25, no. 4 (April 1986), pp. 18–22.

Feigenbaum, Armand V. "America on the Threshold of Quality." *Quality* 29, no. 1 (January 1990), pp. 16–18.

CHAPTER 8

KAORU ISHIKAWA

BRIEF BIOGRAPHY

Kaoru Ishikawa was born in 1915, and earned a degree in applied chemistry from the University of Tokyo in 1939. After the war he became involved in JUSE's fledgling efforts to promote quality. Later he became president of the Musashi Institute of Technology. Until his death in 1989, Dr. Ishikawa was the foremost figure in Japan regarding quality control. He was the first to use the term *total quality control,* and developed the "Seven Tools" that he thought any worker could use. He felt that this distinguished him from other approaches, which he thought placed quality in the hands of specialists. He received many awards during his life, including the Deming Prize and the Second Order of the Sacred Treasure, a very high honor from the Japanese government.

BASIC TENETS

The Seven Tools of Ishikawa are:
1. Pareto charts.
2. Cause-effect diagrams (fishbone or Ishikawa diagrams).
3. Histograms.
4. Check sheets.
5. Scatter diagrams.
6. Flowcharts.
7. Control charts.

These are all discussed in their own chapters and sections in Part 4, Tools and Techniques (histograms and scatter diagrams are both found in the section "Data Presentation," Chapter 16). While Ishikawa realized that not all problems could be solved by these tools, he felt that 95 percent could be, and that any factory worker could effectively use them. While some of the tools had been well known for some time, Ishikawa organized them specifically to improve quality control. Ishikawa originated the cause-effect diagram, descriptively called the *fishbone diagram,* and sometimes called the *Ishikawa diagram* to distinguish it from a different form of cause-effect diagram used in computer programming.

Perhaps the most far reaching of the tools was the idea of a quality control (QC) circle. Its success surprised even him, especially when exported beyond the shores of Japan. He assumed that any country which did not have a Buddhist/Confucian tradition would be inhospitable to QC circles. Today there are over 250,000 QC circles registered with Japan's QC Circle Headquarters, and more than 3,500 case study reports have been filed. This essential aspect of Quality Management was responsible for much of the increase in quality of Japanese products during the past three decades. Ishikawa sees that QC circles are more important to service industries than to manufacturing, since they work much closer to the customer.

ISHIKAWA'S QUALITY PHILOSOPHY

As industry progresses and the level of civilization rises, quality control becomes increasingly important. Some basic tenets of Ishikawa's quality philosophy are summarized here:

1. Quality begins with education and ends with education.
2. The first step in quality is to know the requirements of customers.
3. The ideal state of quality control is when inspection is no longer necessary.
4. Remove the root cause, and not the symptoms.
5. Quality control is the responsibility of all workers and all divisions.
6. Do not confuse the means with the objectives.
7. Put quality first and set your sights on long-term profits.
8. Marketing is the entrance and exit of quality.
9. Top management must not show anger when facts are presented by subordinates.
10. Ninety-five percent of the problems in a company can be solved by the seven tools of quality control.
11. Data without dispersion information (Chapter 20) is false data—for example, stating an average without supplying the standard deviation.

BIBLIOGRAPHY

Ishikawa, Kaoru. *Guide to Quality Control*. 2nd rev. ed. White Plains, N.Y.: UNIPUB–Kraus International, 1976.

Ishikawa, Kaoru. *Quality Control Circles at Work*. Tokyo: JUSE, 1984.

Ishikawa, Kaoru. *What Is Total Quality Control? The Japanese Way*. Englewood Cliffs, N.J.: Prentice Hall, 1985.

CHAPTER 9

JOSEPH M. JURAN*

BRIEF BIOGRAPHY

Joseph M. Juran was born in 1904 in Romania, and came to the United States in 1912. A holder of degrees in engineering and law, he advanced to the positions of quality manager at Western Electric Company, government administrator and professor of engineering at New York University before embarking on a consulting career in 1950. Juran is regarded as one of the architects of the quality revolution in Japan, where he lectured and consulted frequently, starting in 1954. However, he feels that the people mainly responsible for the Japanese quality revolution have been the Japanese operating managers and quality specialists. In 1979, he founded the Juran Institute, which conducts quality training seminars and publishes quality-related works.

BASIC TENETS

Juran defines quality as consisting of two different, though related concepts:

>One form of quality is income oriented, and consists of those features of the product which meet customer needs and thereby produce income. In this sense higher quality usually costs more.
>
>A second form of quality is cost oriented and consists of freedom from failures and deficiencies. In this sense higher quality usually costs less.

Juran points out that managing for quality involves three basic managerial processes: quality planning, quality control, and quality improvement. (These processes parallel those long used to manage for finance.) His "Trilogy," Figure 9–1, shows how these processes are interrelated.

---

*The authors would like to thank Dr. Juran for his review and comments on this chapter.

FIGURE 9-1
Juran's Trilogy

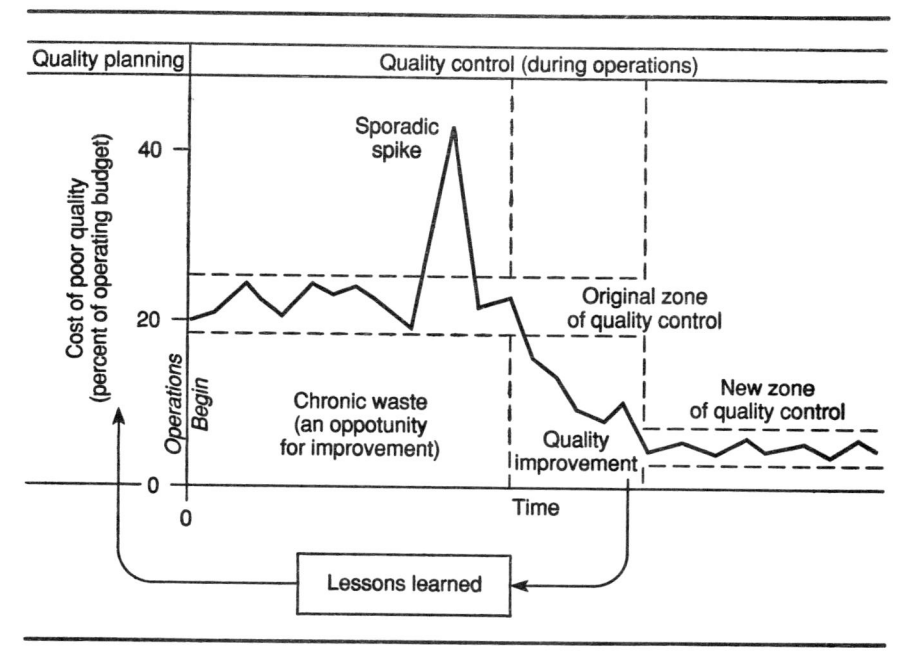

Quality planning	Quality control (during operations)

Y-axis: Cost of poor quality (percent of operating budget), 0 to 40
X-axis: Time

Labels on chart: Sporadic spike; Operations Begin; Chronic waste (an oppotunity for improvement); Original zone of quality control; Quality improvement; New zone of quality control; Lessons learned

Juran identifies the ingredients of the Japanese quality revolution as follows:

1. The upper managers took charge of managing for quality.
2. They trained the entire hierarchy in the processes of managing for quality.
3. They undertook to improve quality at a revolutionary rate.
4. They provided for work force participation.
5. They added quality goals to the business plan.

Juran feels that the United States and other Western countries should adopt similar strategies in order to attain and retain world-class quality status.

JURAN'S APPROACH TO QUALITY IMPROVEMENT

In Juran's priority list, quality improvement comes first. He has a structured approach for this, which he first set out in his book *Managerial Breakthrough*

in 1964. This approach includes a list of nondelegable responsibilities for the upper managers:
1. Create awareness of the need and opportunity for improvement.
2. Mandate quality improvement; make it a part of every job description.
3. Create the infrastructure: establish a quality council; select projects for improvement; appoint teams; provide facilitators.
4. Provide training in how to improve quality.
5. Review progress regularly.
6. Give recognition to the winning teams.
7. Propagandize the results.
8. Revise the reward system to enforce the rate of improvement.
9. Maintain momentum by enlarging the business plan to include goals for quality improvement.

In Juran's view a major, long neglected opportunity for improvement lies in the business processes.

JURAN'S APPROACH TO QUALITY PLANNING

Juran also has identified a universal process for planning to meet quality goals:
1. Identify the customers. Anyone who will be impacted is a customer, whether external or internal.
2. Determine the customers' needs.
3. Create product features which can meet the customers' needs.
4. Create processes which are capable of producing the product features under operating conditions.
5. Transfer the processes to the operating forces.

Juran feels that quality planning should provide for participation by those who will be impacted by the plan. In addition, those who plan should be trained in the use of modern methods and tools of quality planning.

JURAN'S APPROACH TO QUALITY CONTROL

Here Juran follows the familiar feedback loop:
1. Evaluate actual performance.

2. Compare actual with the goal.
3. Take action on the difference.

Juran favors delegating control to the lowest levels in the company through putting workers into a state of self-control. He also favors training workers in data collection and analysis to enable them to make decisions based on facts.

JURAN AND TOTAL QUALITY MANAGEMENT (TQM)

Juran is a strong proponent of TQM. He defines TQM as a collection of certain quality related activities:

1. Quality becomes a part of each upper management agenda.
2. Quality goals enter the business plan.
3. Stretch goals are derived from benchmarking: focus is on the customer and on meeting competition; there are goals for annual quality improvement.
4. Goals are deployed to the action levels.
5. Training is done at all levels.
6. Measurement is established throughout.
7. Upper managers regularly review progress against goals.
8. Recognition is given for superior performance.
9. The reward system is revised.

JURAN'S VIEWS ON WORKER PARTICIPATION

Juran takes a dim view of campaigns to exhort workers to solve the company's quality problems. He discovered many decades ago that over 85 percent of quality problems had their origin in the managerial processes.

Juran feels that the Taylor (Part 3 introduction) system of separating planning from execution has largely become obsolete due to the dramatic rise in worker education. This same rise now makes it possible to delegate to workers many functions previously carried out by planners and supervisors. He feels that the Taylor system should be replaced, and favors experimenting with various options such as: self-control, self-inspection, self-supervision, and self-directing teams of workers.

He believes that self-directing teams of workers will most likely become the dominant form of successor to the Taylor system.

JURAN ON OTHER MAJOR ISSUES

In Juran's view certain major practices of the past should undergo extensive change:
1. The product development cycle should be shortened through participative planning, concurrent engineering, and training the planners in the methods and tools of managing for quality.
2. Supplier relations should be revised. The number of suppliers should be reduced. A teamwork relation should be established with the survivors, based on mutual trust. The traditional adversary approach should be abolished. The duration of contracts should be increased.
3. Training should become results oriented rather than tool oriented. The main purpose of training should be to change behavior rather than to educate. For example training in quality improvement should be preceded by assignment to an improvement project. The training mission should then be to help the team complete the project.

BIBLIOGRAPHY

Juran, J. M. *Managerial Breakthrough*. New York: McGraw-Hill, 1964.

Juran, J. M. and Frank M. Gryna, Jr. *Quality Planning and Analysis*. New York: McGraw-Hill, 1980.

Juran, J. M. *Juran on Quality Improvement Workbook*. New York: Juran Enterprises, 1981.

Juran, J. M. *Quality Control Handbook*. New York: McGraw-Hill, 1988.

Juran, J. M. *Juran on Planning for Quality.* New York: Free Press, 1988.

CHAPTER 10

TOM PETERS

BRIEF BIOGRAPHY

Thomas J. Peters was born in Baltimore, Maryland. Peters has a B.C.E. and M.C.E. in civil engineering, and an M.B.A. and Ph.D. in business from Stanford University. He was a principal of the consulting firm McKinsey & Company, and later established his own consulting firm, Palo Alto Consulting Center. He presently writes a syndicated newspaper column and is a regular commentator on the "McNeil/Lehrer News Hour" on PBS.

BASIC TENETS

Tom Peters is the consummate chronicler of excellence in business. His first work, *In Search of Excellence,* was a major best seller. Peters takes an empirical approach to Quality Management. He is interested in what has worked for whom, and why it was successful. This makes for highly absorbing and inspirational reading. Some have criticized this approach as being primarily anecdotal in nature, and lacking a strong framework. Peters has attempted an answer to these charges in his third work, *Thriving on Chaos: Handbook for Management Revolution.* In this work he provides 45 specific prescriptions in transforming an organization. These points are summarized below, as are the nine primary observations from *In Search of Excellence.*

NINE ASPECTS OF EXCELLENT COMPANIES

1. Managing ambiguity and paradox. Chaos is the rule of businesses, not the exception. The business climate is always uncertain and always ambiguous. The rational, numerical approach does not always work because we live in irrational times.

2. A bias for action. Do it, try it, fix it. The point is to try something, without fear of failure. Sochiro Honda, founder of Honda, said that only 1 out of 100 of his ideas worked. Fortunately for him, he kept trying after his 99th failure.

3. Close to the customer. Excellent companies have an almost uncanny feel for what their customer wants. This is because they are a customer of their own product, or they closely listen to their customer.

4. Autonomy and entrepreneurship. Ownership of a department, tasking, or problem is essential in motivating employees. It is the most cited reason for entering into self-employment. Excellent companies allow and encourage autonomy and within company entrepreneurship.

5. Productivity through people. Not surprisingly, people act in accordance with their treatment. Treat them as being untrustworthy, and they will be. Treat them as business partners, and they will be. Excellent companies have taken the leap of faith required to trust your employees to do the right thing right.

6. Hands-on, value-driven. Practice management by walking around. Constantly ask what the value added is of every process and procedure.

7. Stick to the knitting. Stay close to the basic industry of your organization. The skills or culture involved in a different industry be may a shock that is fatal to the organization.

8. Simple form, lean staff. Flat organizations unencumbered by a heavy headquarters characterized the excellent companies.

9. Loose-tight properties. Tight control is maintained while at the same time allowing staff far more flexibility than is the norm.

PETERS'S PRESCRIPTIONS FOR MANAGEMENT REVOLUTION

1. Create total customer responsiveness. Customer responsiveness requires listening to the customer at every available opportunity. Be extraordinarily responsive. Create a niche and differentiate your product from your competitors.

2. Pursue fast-paced innovation. Never let up on innovating new projects. Don't be concerned over failure, and don't worry about being original. If failure occurs, make it happen quickly.

3. Empower people. Trust your people. Train them. Use self-managing teams, involving everyone in everything. Eliminate management by fear and edict.

4. Love change. Create a vision and demonstrate this vision by example. Delegate authority to the lowest practical level.

5. Rebuild systems for a chaotic world. Revise and reexamine what is measured. Decentralize information, providing it in real time to those who need it to perform better. Set conservative goals and demand integrity.

BIBLIOGRAPHY

Peters, Thomas J., and Robert H. Waterman, Jr. *In Search of Excellence.* New York: Harper & Row, 1982.

Peters, Thomas J., and Nancy Austin, *A Passion for Excellence.* New York: Random House, 1985.

Peters, Thomas J. "It's Time to Get Back to Basics." *Quality,* May 1986, pp. 14–20.

Peters, Thomas J. *Thriving on Chaos: Handbook for Management Revolution.* New York: Alfred A. Knopf, 1987.

CHAPTER 11

GENICHI TAGUCHI

BRIEF BIOGRAPHY

Genichi Taguchi is a four-time winner of the Deming Prize in Japan. He received the first award ever given, in 1960, for the development of practical statistical theory. Dr. Taguchi worked for Nippon Telegraph and Telephone. While controversial, many companies have used his ideas to advantage in designing experiments and reducing process and product variation. His son, Shin Taguchi, carries on his father's work at the American Supplier Institute in Dearborn, Michigan.

BASIC TENETS

Taguchi's philosophy involves the entire manufacturing function from design through manufacture. His methods focus on the customer by using the loss function (Figure 11–1). Taguchi describes quality in terms of the loss generated by that product to society. This loss to society can be from the time a product is shipped until the end of its useful life. The loss is measured in dollars and therefore allows engineers to communicate to nonengineers the magnitude of this loss in a recognizable, common term. This is sometimes referred to as a *bilingual* mode, meaning that one can talk to upper-level managers in terms of dollars, and to engineers and those who work on the product or service in terms of things, hours, pounds, and so on. With the loss function, the engineer is able to communicate in the language of things and the language of money.

> The key to loss reduction is not meeting specifications, but reducing variance from the nominal or target value.

The Taguchi method has been described as *the most powerful tool* for achieving quality improvements, according to Jim Pratt, director of ITT's statistical programs. Pratt estimates that ITT saved some $60 million in an 18-month period.

FIGURE 11-1
The Loss Function

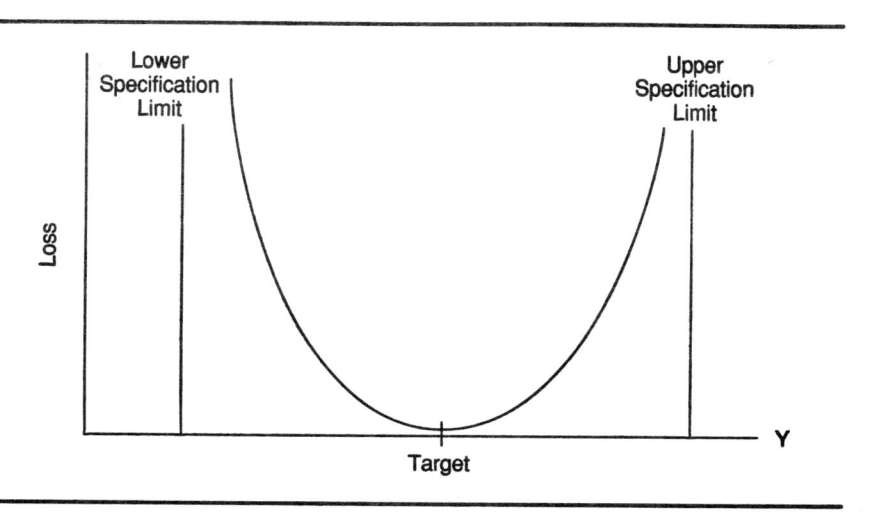

```
         Lower                          Upper
      Specification                  Specification
         Limit                           Limit

Loss


                         Target                      Y
```

Many practitioners of Taguchi methods in this country feel that the on-line quality control practices described below will eventually supplant statistical quality control as it has to a large extent in Japan.

An overview of Taguchi's quality philosophy is provided below.

TAGUCHI'S QUALITY PHILOSOPHY

1. An important dimension of the quality of a manufactured product is the total loss generated by that product to society.
2. In a competitive economy, continuous quality improvement and cost reduction are necessary to stay in business.
3. A continuous quality improvement program includes incessant reduction in the variation of product performance characteristics about their target values.
4. The customer's loss due to a product performance variation is often approximately proportional to the square of the deviation of the performance characteristics from its target value. Thus, a quality measure quickly degrades with large deviation from the target.
5. The final quality and cost of a manufactured product are determined to a large extent by the engineering designs of the product and its manufacturing process.

6. A performance variation can be reduced by exploiting the nonlinear effects of the product (or process) parameters on the performance characteristic.
7. Statistically planned experiments can be used to identify the settings of product (and process) parameters that reduce performance variation.

ON-LINE AND OFF-LINE QUALITY CONTROL

Taguchi methods of off-line and on-line quality control provide a unique approach to reducing product variation. On-line methods include the various techniques of maintaining target values and the variation about the target in the manufacturing environment. These techniques would include such methods as statistical control charts. It is the off-line quality control techniques that make the Taguchi methods distinctive. Off-line quality control involves the design or quality engineering function and consists of three components:

System design. System design is the selection and design of a product that will satisfy the requirements of the customer. The design should be functional and robust[1] to changes in environmental conditions during service. The product should have minimal variation and should provide the most value for the price. Additionally the product should provide minimal functional variation due to use factors such as wear. The techniques employed here are various methods of establishing customer requirements and translating those requirements into engineering terms. Quality Function Deployment methods and the loss function are often employed in system design.

Parameter design. Parameter design is the identification of key process variables that affect product variation and the establishment of parameter levels that will impart the least amount of variation into the product's function. This is accomplished through the use of statistical experimental designs. Taguchi methods depart somewhat from classical experimental design in that the Taguchi approach uses only a small fraction of all possible experimental combinations and extracts the "right" conditions in a very efficient manner.

Tolerance design. Tolerance design is the determination of which factors contribute the most to end product variation and the establishment of the appropriate tolerances for those factors required to bring the final product

---

[1] A product is said to be robust when it has a lower degree of sensitivity to variation within the manufacturing process, although quality controls try to minimize variation.

into specification. Tolerance design is used only if the product variability is not confined to some "tolerable" level. The advantage of these methods is efficiency; rather than tightening tolerances across the board, only those that will have the most impact are tightened.

These three functions may be thought of as the definition of quality, the design engineering of quality, and the engineering of the production process. The traditional approach has been to design a product more or less independently of the manufacturing processes, and then to go about the reduction of variability in those processes to enhance the product quality. Taguchi methods attempt to design products that are robust to variation in the manufacturing process.

This requires analyzing two variables that can affect the performance of the product or process: design parameters and noise. The design parameters can be selected by the engineer. Such a parameter forms a design specification.

The noise consists of all those variables that cause the design parameter to deviate from the target value. Whether these noise causes are assignable is of small importance. Noise that can be identified should be included as an element in the experiment. Outer noise is caused by such things as variation in operating environments and human errors. Inner noise is caused by such things as deterioration. Between product noise is caused by manufacturing imperfections. Outer and inner noise is controllable by off-line methods such as parameter design. Between product noise can be controlled by on-line and off-line techniques.

The point of the experiment is to identify the parameter settings at which the results of noise are minimal. Through development of a design parameter matrix and a noise matrix, either physical experiments or computer simulations may be conducted to determine optimal settings of design parameters. Orthogonal arrays (see Chapter 20, Design of Experiments section) are suggested for constructing the matrices. These arrays are eventually used to determine signal-to-noise ratios as performance statistics.

Successes have been achieved using these techniques (see Schmidt's work and almost any issue of *Technometrics*), their application is somewhat controversial, and demands a specialist in statistics. Some of the technique is still being formulated in detail. Despite the apparent technical complexity, the design of experiments methodology provides a rich framework upon which to base quality and producibility determinations.

According to Raghu Kackar (an advocate and articulator of the Taguchi method), the four primary reasons for using statistically planned industrial experiments are:

1. To identify settings of design parameters at which the effect of the noise source on performance characteristics is minimized.
2. To identify settings of design parameters that reduce cost without impairing quality.

3. To identify parameters that have a large influence on the mean value of the performance characteristic but have no effect on its variation.
4. To identify parameters which have no detectable influence on performance characteristics and on which tolerances can be relaxed.

BIBLIOGRAPHY

Kackar, Raghu N. "Off-Line Quality Control, Parameter Design, and the Taguchi Method." *Journal of Quality Technology* 17, no. 4 (October 1985), pp. 176–209.

Kackar, Raghu N. "Taguchi's Quality Philosophy: Analysis and Commentary." *Quality Progress* 19, no. 12 (December 1986), pp. 21–29.

Kackar, Raghu N. "Quality Planning for Service Industries." *Quality Progress* 21, no. 8. (August 1988), pp. 39–42.

Schmidt, Michael S., and Larry C. Meile. "Taguchi Designs and Linear Programming Speed New Product Formulation." *Interfaces* 19, no. 5 (September/October 1989), pp. 49–56.

Taguchi, Genichi. *Introduction to Quality Engineering*. Dearborn, Mich.: American Supplier Institute Inc., 1986.

Taguchi, Genichi. *System of Experimental Design*. Dearborn, Mich.: American Supplier Institute, 1987.

Taguchi, Genichi and Don Clausing. "Robust Quality." *Harvard Business Review*, January/February 1990, pp. 65–75.

Taguchi, Genichi, and Yu-In Wu. *Introduction to Off-Line Quality Control Systems*. Central Quality Control Association, 1980.

CHAPTER 12

HISTORICAL MASTERS

INTRODUCTION

The phrase *historical masters* may bring to mind such leading quality figures of the early part of the 20th century such as Shewhart, creator of control charts. The group of scientists who developed quality control at AT&T in the first quarter century are often cited as *the originators* of quality. While this may be true of 20th-century United States, it certainly is not true worldwide. China had quality standards some 2,000 years or more ago. If we broaden our search for "original" Quality Management masters, and engage in some divergent thinking (Chapter 15, Creativity and Innovation section), where should we start?

Surely the first quality engineer was some unknown chariot maker in Sumeria who observed that the smoother the wheel, the faster the chariot, or some swordsmith farther north in the land of the Hittites who scrutinized his work in order to free it of all blemishes, thereby increasing its cutting power. Or was it a Neanderthal, who plied his craft with flint knapping tools, being attentive and conscientious in shaping a tool for a precise use? Modern archaeologists have demonstrated that these skills are difficult to acquire. Yet we know that the skills were practiced by Neanderthals and were passed on through generations. So perhaps quality control predates *Homo sapiens,* and originated with *Homo sapiens neanderthalensis.*

While this *gedanken* (thought experiment) is entertaining, we have no written record to guide us. Written history, however, provides a grand procession of characters and legends to emulate and avoid. Some would seem to presage Total Quality Management principles. While others can undoubtedly be found[1] from nearly every era and area, the spotlight here will be on three of the authors' favorites: Sun-Tzu, Aesop, and Socrates.

---

[1] Clemens and Mayer's work, *The Classic Touch: Leadership Lessons from Homer to Hemingway,* dispenses management lessons from historical figures, and provides a diverting outlook.

SUN-TZU

Sun-Tzu lived sometime during the warring states period (480–221 B.C.) in China. During this time, the entire world, as the Chinese knew it, was in constant war. Sun-Tzu observed the political and leadership struggles and attempted to codify how best to approach these disciplines. An analogy has been made between Sun-Tzu's process and those of the immune system[2]: it wards off disease and attackers without damaging the underlying support system. In this respect it also embodies principles of TQM: survival, growth, and continuous improvement in a chaotic world.

The work is only some 5,600 words long, and can be read easily in an evening. There are a number of excellent translations in English, most notably the one by Samuel B. Griffith. A novel translation, by R. L. Wing, casts the terminology into business and strategic terms rather than martial terms. Wing also gives extensive commentary on applying these principles to one's daily life and work life.

Sun-Tzu's work has 13 sections, summarized below:

1. Calculations. Is the goal reasonable and worthwhile? If so then the time to act is now. If not, wait and build strength until it is reasonable. Self-reflection (e.g., benchmarking and audits) are necessary to understand one's own strength as well as that of the enemy. Both the self and the enemy must be understood.

2. Estimating the cost. Contingencies and alternatives must be weighed. Once the costs have been estimated, then commit to an unrelenting forward momentum. There must be unbelievably swift and decisive action, with no looking back.

3. Plan of attack. Is the thing isolated or integral? If the objective is isolated, then a forward attack is appropriate. If it is integral, then a broader, less obvious attack route may be necessary.

4. Positioning. Remove elements around you that allow backsliding. One must have a supportive environment. You cannot cross a river by going across halfway and then returning to shore to rest for the next half.

---

[2]Like the immune system, which can enter an autoimmune phase and destroy the very body it was protecting, so too can Quality Management consume its own as it metamorphoses a company via continuous change and quality improvement, making the new business very different from the old business.

5. Directing—Positioning your foe. Isolate your foe, make plans that do not include it; enlist the help of others. Act spontaneously.

6. Illusion and reality. The opponent must not be allowed to rest. When weak, feign strength. When strong, feign weakness.

7. Maneuvers and tactics. Indirect tactics such as logistics are essential to success. Indirect actions which lead to direct effect are the best. Competition within your own forces is dangerous. The focus must be on the enemy. Give your opponents the ability to flee. Damage the overtaken as little as possible. They are tomorrow's customers.

8. Spontaneity in the field. Sun-Tzu warns against being overly cautious, reckless, angry, fastidious, and attached to the organization or the status quo.

9. Moving the force—Confrontation. Self-control and discipline will grow from a determined challenge.

10. Situational positioning. Challenge only when certain. Put yourself between your foe and his support system, as disorder brings defeat.

11. The nine situations. Awareness of the situation is vital. Contradictory situations call for contradictory action.

12. The fiery attack. Do not prolong the confrontation. Enlist help from the outside and make every action count.

13. The use of intelligence. Information is the essence of success or defeat.

AESOP

Aesop was (perhaps) a Greek slave who lived in the 6th century B.C. While not providing the integrated framework of Sun-Tzu, Aesop's simple fables or parables provide profound insight into the nature of people's conduct in society. What is so instructive is that little has changed in human nature since the beginnings of civilization. Aesop has permeated Western literature for some 500 years, as browsing through a quotation dictionary will readily confirm. A small sample of Quality Management related morals is presented:

United we stand, divided we fall. **The four oxen and the lion.** A direct appeal to the use of self-managing teams, quality circles, and other uses of teamwork and shared vision.

Please all, and you please none. **The man, the boy, and the donkey.** A vision that has been defined in scope and is attainable is essential. Serving some segments of customers may mean ignoring others.

A liar will not be believed, even when he speaks the truth (cry wolf). **The shepard boy.** Credibility in management is regained everyday, and when lost, it may be lost until that management is replaced, and quite likely even longer. Trust is not bought by salary, or enforced by memos. Without trust, it is difficult to achieve the union required to succeed.

We often despise what is most useful to us. **The hart and the hunter.** Exempt, nonexempt, suits, Joe Punchclock, . . . the list is long that we use to demean the workers on whom we rely. As Martin Luther King, Jr., said, there is dignity in all work. Failure to understand this leads to strikes, lockouts and boycotts, and management by fear.

You may share the labor of the great, but not the spoils. **The lion's share.** Rewards must be given out on a fair and regular basis, and it must be understood how one can achieve these rewards.

Perseverance wins the race. **The hare and the tortoise.** Aesop agrees with Sun-Tzu regarding careful calculations, plotting, and provisioning. Ambition and excitable energy are no substitute for wisdom and cunning.

SOCRATES

Socrates, the philosophizing stonemason, lived from 470 B.C. to 399 B.C., in Athens, during the Golden Age of Pericles. He is known to us from the works of Plato as a one of the greatest philosophers. A number of Quality Management concepts can be found in the various Socratic dialogues.

Root cause analysis. Socrates was always asking Why?, and even when told why, would keep probing until he reached the bottommost cause.

This rumination was meant to sweep away preconceptions and prejudices to reach the real reasons or truths of whatever subject was before him.

Empowering the worker. Democracy lends voice to all. Coupled with critical self-examination, this leads to an empowering force of continuous self-improvement.

Vision and ethics. "The unexamined life is not worth living" is a quote of Plato and Socrates. Constantly examining our beliefs and motives requires building a solid framework of morals and ethics.

Management by walking around. "Socratic Dialogue" refers to a technique of asking questions so that those answering them will be led to the answer. It is difficult to craft such questions, but it is highly rewarding for teacher and student alike. Socrates considered himself a gadfly, always goading others into thinking about their actions and beliefs.

BIBLIOGRAPHY

Aesop. *Fables.* (Numerous translations available.)

Clemens, John K., and Douglas F. Mayer. *The Classic Touch: Leadership Lessons from Homer to Hemingway.* Homewood, Ill.: Dow Jones-Irwin, 1987.

Griffin, Gerald R. *Machiavelli on Management.* New York: Praeger Publishers, 1991.

Juran, J. M. "China's Ancient History of Managing for Quality." *Quality Progress* 23, no. 7 (July 1990), pp. 31–35.

Sun-Tzu. *The Art of War.* trans. Samuel B. Griffith. London: Oxford University Press, 1963.

Sun-Tzu. *The Art of Strategy.* trans. R. L. Wing. New York: Dolphin/Doubleday, 1988.

Plato. *The Republic.* (Numerous translations available.)